THE COOK'S HANDBOOK

Marika Hanbury Tenison was born in London in 1938. She is a well-known authority on cooking and is cookery editor of the UK *Sunday Telegraph* and *Spectator*. She regularly contributes to other leading journals and makes frequent television and radio broadcasts.

She lives on a farm on Bodmin Moor in Cornwall with her husband, explorer Robin Hanbury Tenison. Their house and garden, including the kitchen, have been featured in *Vogue*, *Ideal Home*, *American House and Garden* and *Freezing Digest*.

Her other cookery books include *Deep Freeze Cookery* (Pan), *Deep Freeze Sense* (Pan), *Left Over for Tomorrow* (Penguin), *Best of British Cooking* (Hart-Davis), *Recipes from a Country Kitchen* (Hart-Davis) and *New Fish Cookery* (Hart-Davis), *Eat Well and be Slim* (Pan) and *Deep Freezing* (Teach Yourself).

TEACH YOURSELF BOOKS

THE COOK'S HANDBOOK

Marika Hanbury Tenison

Illustrated by Vanessa Pancheri

TEACH YOURSELF BOOKS
Hodder and Stoughton

First Impression 1980

Published in the USA by David McKay & Co. Inc.,
750 Third Avenue, New York, NY 10017, USA.

British Library Cataloguing in Publication Data

Hanbury-Tenison, Marika
The cook's handbook.
1. Cookery
I. Title
641.5 TX652

ISBN 0–340–24710–X

Printed and bound in Great Britain for Hodder and Stoughton paperbacks, a division of Hodder and Stoughton Ltd, Mill Road, Dunton Green, Sevenoaks, Kent, (Editorial Office; 47 Bedford Square, London, WC1B 3DP) by
Richard Clay (The Chaucer Press) Ltd., Bungay, Suffolk

With thanks to Joan who clears up all the mess, actually says she enjoys it and also that she is learning.

Contents

Conversion Tables

WEIGHTS

½ oz	10 g (grams)
1	25
1½	40
2	50
2½	60
3	75
4	110
4½	125
5	150
6	175
7	200
8	225
9	250
10	275
12	350
1 lb	450
1½	700
2	900
3	1 kg 350 g

VOLUME

2 fl oz	55 ml
3 fl oz	75
5 fl oz (¼ pint)	150
½ pint	275
¾ pint	425
1 pint	570
1¾ pints	1 litre

(2 pint basin = 1 litre)

TEMPERATURES

Mark 1	275°F	140°C
2	300	150
3	325	170
4	350	180
5	375	190
6	400	200
7	425	220
8	450	230

MEASUREMENTS

⅛ in	3 mm (millimetre)
¼ in	0·5 cm (centimetre)
½	1
¾	2
1	2·5
1¼	3
1½	4
1¾	4·5
2	5
3	7·5
4	10
5	13
6	15
7	18
8	20
9	23
10	25·5
11	28
12	30

All these are *approximate* conversions, which have been either rounded up or down. In a few recipes it has been necessary to modify them very slightly.

You must either follow Metric or Imperial measurements. Do not mix both in one recipe.

Foreword

Many cookery books, even for the beginner cook, tend to leave out some of the basic preparations or principles of cooking which the new cook may not know. This book is intended to fill that gap.

It is a book which will be handy for all cooks, however experienced, to have near them in the kitchen at all times, not only to provide that basic knowledge which may be missing but also, I hope, to give ideas for new dishes.

There is no magic about cooking. Good cooking stems from an interest in food and the pleasure it gives; once you get the general idea and know how to make a few of the basic recipes you will find that the rest quickly falls into place. Almost all recipes, however involved they may seem at first glance, stem from one basic and simple starting point with additions that may be drawn from other equally simple beginnings.

Few of us can remember everything we read and learn and that is why I hope this book may be of help to all those beginning on the exciting path to cookery. And remember that cooking is not a skill you are born with or need to start at an early age; anyone can cook well providing they can read a cookery book and realise that cooking is not just a chore but that it should also be an enjoyment to oneself and a great pleasure to others.

Marika Hanbury Tenison
Maidenwell 1979

Alphabet of Basic Cooking Terms

Although I have tried to keep the cookery terms used in this book to those that are simple and in everyday general use, I felt it would be useful to include a short glossary of cookery terms that you are likely to find both in this book and in some more sophisticated recipes.

Aspic jelly A clear savoury jelly made from clarified stock or aspic crystals and used for setting and garnishing cold savoury dishes.

Au gratin A French term for a dish which is finished with a sauce, sprinkled with breadcrumbs or a mixture of breadcrumbs and cheese and browned in a hot oven or under a grill before serving. Plain dishes like cauliflower cheese or macaroni cheese often benefit enormously by this quick, last minute, touch.

Bain marie (water bath) A French term for a vessel, usually a baking tin, half filled with water that is kept just below boiling point. Soups and sauces are kept warm in this water without being allowed to continue cooking and the principle is also used when baking dishes such as egg custards and pâtés.

Baking Cooking in an oven without liquid or fat, i.e. baked potatoes, bread, cakes etc.

Baking blind Cooking a pastry case without a filling so that a flan or tart case will remain crisp when the filling is added. Line a case with pastry. Cut some foil or greaseproof paper the same size as the case and press the lining into the sides and bottom of the case. Fill with dried beans, rusks of bread or small metal beans, available for the purpose, before baking.

Barding Covering the breast of poultry or other lean meat with fat to prevent them drying out during cooking.

Basting An important part of almost any roasting recipe. Liquid, fat or juices from the pan are poured over the meat, poultry or game at regular intervals during the cooking time to prevent the ingredients drying out.

Beating Agitating ingredients by means of a fork, whisk, rotary or wire whisk to incorporate ingredients or to increase them in volume.

Béchamel One of the classic French white sauces which forms the base of many other sauces.

Beurre manié A mixture of flour and butter beaten together until smooth and added to soups or sauces to thicken them after they have been cooked. The mixture is whisked into the hot liquid and simmered until the liquid thickens. Very useful for thickening recipes which do not seem to have reached the required consistency.

Binding Adding some form of liquid to dry ingredients in order to consolidate them.

Blanching Plunging raw ingredients into boiling water or putting them in cold water and then bringing them to the boil. This is used to whiten ingredients, loosen the skin of fruit and vegetables, prevent ingredients from discolouring and, in the case of freezing, to destroy bacteria.

Blending Mixing ingredients together by a smooth motion using a spoon or spatula.

Boiling Cooking liquid at over 100°C (212°F) so that bubbles are breaking on the surface of the liquid all the time the ingredients are being cooked.

Bouquet garni A French term for a mixture of herbs that is added for flavouring to many casseroles, stews and soups. The combination of herbs can vary according to the ingredients used in the dish but the simplest of all is a bunch consisting of a sprig of parsley, a sprig of thyme and a bay leaf. The herbs are tied together, added to the dish for cooking and then removed before serving. In a more complicated *bouquet garni* garlic, cloves and sometimes other spices are added and tied in a piece of muslin for cooking.

Braising Ingredients cooked in the oven with enough liquid to prevent them drying. Meat and poultry that are not tender enough are cooked in a covered pan to prevent evaporation and often combined with vegetables. Basting is not usually necessary for foods that are to be braised. Braising is also used for cooking a great many varieties of vegetables on their own.

Brining Covering meat, fish or vegetables with a salt and water solution in order to prolong their life.

Brochette French term for ingredients cooked on skewers.

Broiling American term for grilling – see *Grilling*.

Browning The process of giving the top of a dish a pleasant, finishing, crisp and golden brown colouring. This is done either under a grill or in a hot oven.

Caramel Sugar slowly heated over a low flame until it melts and is slightly burnt. Caramel is used for flavouring sweets, for lining pudding moulds and also, when it is allowed to become a deep brown in colour, for colouring some rich stews.

Casserole The name given to a heavy, fireproof dish with a tight fitting lid and to the dishes which are cooked in it. Casseroling is usually applied to meat or poultry combined with vegetables and cooked slowly to allow all the flavours to develop and the meat to be very tender.

Chilling Cooling foods by leaving them in a refrigerator until they are completely cold.

Chopping Cutting food with a sharp knife into small even pieces. An onion *finely* chopped will be the size of coarsely grated cheese; if a recipe calls for the onion to be coarsely chopped it should be cut into flakes the size of a small fingernail.

Clarifying Clearing or purifying liquids or fats of large particles or impurities.

Coating Covering food for frying with an even layer of seasoned flour, beaten egg and dried breadcrumbs or with batter. The term is also applied for masking food with a cold or hot sauce.

Cocotte (or *ramekin*) A small dish for cooking individual eggs.

Colander A metal bowl or basket perforated with holes for draining.

Cornflour The starch of maize, very finely ground to a powder and used mainly for thickening.

Cornstarch American term for cornflour.

Creaming A term used to describe beating fat and sugar together until they reach the consistency of lightly whipped cream and the sugar has dissolved. Usually used in cake-making.

Crimping The method of pinching the edges of pastry together to ensure an airtight seal and to give an attractive fluted effect.
Croquette French for a mixture of ingredients, usually cooked, which are bound together, shaped into sausage forms, coated with egg and breadcrumbs and deep fried.
Croûtons French for small cubes of bread which are deep fried and served with soups.
Curdle Used to describe mixtures which have separated. Cream will curdle if it is boiled; milk will curdle if an acid ingredient like lemon is added to it and mayonnaise will curdle if oil is added to the egg yolks too quickly.
Curing An alternative word for preserving ingredients by drying, salting or smoking. Smoked mackerel is sometimes referred to as 'cured mackerel'.
Deep-fat frying Cooking ingredients in more than six inches of fat or oil so that they are totally immersed during cooking.
Dough Uncooked mixtures based on flour, bread, pastry and scone mixes etc.
Draw To remove the intestines of a bird. A drawn bird is ready for cooking.
Dredging or *dusting* Covering food lightly with a dry ingredient such as sugar or flour. Not to be confused with 'coat' where the ingredients are completely covered with flour.
Dress or *dressed* The term applied to a piece of meat, game or poultry which is prepared ready for cooking.
En croûte French for a dish of meat, fish or other ingredients which is wrapped in pastry before being cooked.
En papillote Ingredients which are wrapped in greaseproof paper or foil to seal in the juices and flavour before being cooked.
Escallopes Thin slices of meat cut from the top of the leg of an animal and very tender.
Farce or *forcemeat* Savoury stuffings used for meat, poultry and vegetables.
Fines herbes A mixture of finely chopped fresh herbs.
Flaking Separating the flesh of cooked fish into flakes.
Flambé Setting light to a dish to seal in flavours or to add the taste of liquor at the last moment. A spirit such as rum, brandy or whisky is heated over a flame, poured over the dish and then allowed to burn out.
Folding in Using a folding movement rather than a stirring or beating one to combine ingredients lightly together when a mixing

rather than an amalgamation is required. Usually done with a fork, metal spoon or a wire whisk using a gentle hand.
Fondue A dish cooked at the table over a spirit flame.
Frying Cooking in a shallow pan in hot fat or oil over a high heat.
Garnishing Decorating dishes using edible ingredients to make them look more appetising and attractive.
Giblets The heart, liver and gizzard of birds, removed before cooking and used mainly for stock.
Gill An English liquid measurement equivalent to ¼ pint or approximately 140 ml.
Glass Usually a measurement of wine or spirit for cooking; a glass measurement equals 8 fl oz or 200 ml.
Glazing Beaten egg, egg white, milk, a syrup or meat glaze brushed over a dish to give a shining appearance.
Grating Shaving food into uniform flakes usually by using a grater. Foods to be grated must be firm and ingredients such as cheese should be on the stale side to make grating efficient.
Grilling Cooking foods by direct overhead heat.
Grinding American term for mincing. Reducing hard ingredients to a coarse or fine powder by using a food mill or electric appliance.
Hanging An important process of hanging meat, poultry or game in a cool place to help develop the flavour and tenderise the taste.
Hors d'oeuvres French for dishes, usually cold, served as a first course or appetiser.
Hulling Removing the stalk and calyx of soft fruit before cooking or serving.
Infusing Pouring hot liquid over herbs or spices to extract their flavour.
Julienne Thin, matchstick thick strips of vegetables used in soups and salads.
Knead Massaging a dough with the knuckles or fingertips to make it smooth.
Larding Small strips of fat (usually bacon or pork fat) are inserted by means of a larding needle into the flesh of meat to add flavour and prevent drying.
Liaison Thickening ingredients usually flour, cornflour etc. slaked with liquid and added to sauces and soups.
Macerating Softening foods in a liquid.
Marinade A mixture of oil, vinegar or wine, seasoning and spices in which meat is soaked to tenderise and flavour. When ingredients are soaking in a marinade they are said to be marinating.

Meunière Ingredients which are cooked over heat in butter. These dishes are usually flavoured with lemon juice, seasoning and parsley.
Mincing Very finely chopped ingredients with a hand or electric machine.
Mirepoix French for a mixture of vegetables and ham or bacon used as a base for braising meat.
Mixed herbs Usually applied to a mixture of dried herbs.
Muslin or cheesecloth Fine gauze cotton used to wrap ingredients to keep dry or to strain ingredients through to obtain a finer consistency than through a wire sieve.
Parboiling Half cooking ingredients by boiling before draining them and cooking by another method.
Pâté A mixture of meats, game, poultry or fish, finely minced, cooked in a terrine or wrapped in pastry to seal in the flavours and served cold.
Pectin An ingredient in fruits and some vegetables which makes ingredients set for jellies and jams.
Perforated spoon A spoon with holes in for lifting solid ingredients out of liquid or fat.
Pimento Red peppers which are preserved and sold in tins or jars.
Piquant Sharp, pungent flavour used to describe sauces.
Pith The white membrane on the inside of citrus fruits such as oranges and lemons.
Plucking Removing the feathers from any poultry or game before cooking.
Poaching Cooking foods at simmering point with enough liquid to cover them.
Pot roasting Cooking food slowly in a small amount of liquid over heat.
Pulping Reducing food to a purée.
Ramekin See *Cocotte*.
Reducing Boiling liquid over a high heat to reduce it in quantity in order to concentrate the flavours.
Rendering Extracting liquid fat from the solid fat of meat or poultry.
Rennet A natural ingredient used for coagulating milk for junket and for making cheeses.
Roasting A method of cooking meat or poultry in the oven, usually basting the ingredients in its own fats and juices.

Roux Equal quantities of fat and flour cooked together to form the basis of a thickening ingredient for soups and sauces.

Rubbing in A term used in pastry making. Fingertips are used to rub fat, cut in small pieces, into flour until the mixture resembles coarse breadcrumbs and is ready for the addition of liquid.

Salting See *Brining*.

Sauté Frying food in shallow rather than deep fat or oil. Usually the food is cooked over a low heat and softened rather than crisped.

Scoring Making shallow cuts with a sharp knife through the skin or fat of an ingredient to speed up cooking or to develop flavours rubbed into the surface.

Searing Cooking ingredients over a high heat by grilling or in a hot oven in order to seal in flavours before continuing to cook.

Seasoned flour Used for coating ingredients and consisting of flour that has been seasoned (or mixed) with salt, pepper and sometimes another seasoning ingredient such as cayenne pepper or paprika pepper etc.

Seasoning Seasoning applies basically to the flavours given to ingredients by adding salt and pepper but it can also include the addition of other ingredients such as spices and herbs to give flavour.

Shredding Cutting or slicing food into very thin slices.

Sieve A metal mesh of varying thicknesses for straining or purée-ing ingredients.

Sieving Passing softened food through a fine mesh sieve in order to give a smooth consistency.

Sifting Shaking ingredients through a sieve to remove any lumps.

Simmering Having brought ingredients to the boil, keeping them at just below boiling point so that the surface of the liquid just moves but doesn't break into bubbles.

Skimming Removing the surface fat or scum from a liquid in order to clarify it.

Soused foods Ingredients which have been pickled in a vinegar or salt solution to preserve them.

Spatula A solid paddle of wood, plastic or metal for stirring, lifting or scraping.

Steaming Cooking foods over steam either in a colander or steamer over boiling water, or in a pudding basin in a little boiling water.

Steeping Pouring boiling water over ingredients to extract their flavourings.

Stewing Cooking combined ingredients in a tightly enclosed vessel over a slow heat or in a slow oven to tenderise them and preserve all their flavours.
Stirring Combining ingredients with a wooden spoon, fork or spatula in a circular motion.
Stock Liquid produced by cooking raw or cooked meat, poultry, fish and vegetable trimmings in liquid, with a bouquet garni and seasonings, and straining. The resulting liquid is used to flavour soups, sauces and gravies.
Straining Separating liquids from ingredients which have been used to flavour them.
Stuffing Sweet or savoury fillings for all manner of ingredients to increase them in bulk or to give them additional flavouring.
Sugar syrup A syrup made by combining sugar and water and heating until the sugar has dissolved and the required consistency is reached; used for sweets and fruit salads.
Sweating to 'sweat' A term usually used to cook vegetables over a low heat in fat or vegetable oil in order to soften them and bring out their flavour.
Terrine A thick earthenware or china dish used for ingredients cooked in such a dish; usually coarse pâtés, potted meats, meat loaves etc.
Thickening Adding body to soups, sauces or stews and casseroles by adding a flour or a liaison of flour and fat or egg yolks and cream beaten together.
Tomato purée A commercial product which gives a strong tomato flavouring to a dish.
Tossing Lifting ingredients off a dish with a spoon and fork to incorporate them or coat them lightly with a sauce or dressing.
Trussing Tying a bird into a compact shape before cooking so that the wings and legs are held closely to the body.
Whipping and whisking Beating air as fast as possible into ingredients by means of hand rotary beater or an electric whisk.
Wire whisk A hand beater made of loops of wire. Especially good for mixing sauces.
Zest The thin coloured skin of citrus fruit which contains a strong oil. The zest of citrus fruit is usually removed with a grater.

Kitchen Equipment

A bad cook should never 'blame her tools'; nevertheless a good cook will know only too well the advantages of cooking with good quality equipment. Using the right tool for the right job, especially when it is well made, speeds up the cooking time and results in a more professional result.

Saucepans and frying pans

There is probably a wider choice of pans from which to choose than any other piece of kitchen equipment. On the whole when choosing your pans I would recommend that you stay away from buying any equipment that, although it may look pretty, tends to be 'gimmicky'. Cast-iron ware is excellent for slow cooking as it heats slowly but then retains the heat; tinned copper pans heat quickly and are much used by professional chefs but they have the disadvantage of being extremely expensive and a problem to keep clean. The best all round saucepans in my opinion are those made from stainless steel with a copper base, which will last well, can be used on all kinds of heat and are reasonably easy to keep clean.

Good saucepans should last a lifetime; look for pans that are relatively heavy for their size and which have tightly fitting lids.

Almost all saucepans can be used on a gas cooker but if you cook on electricity it is essential to have a heavy pan to distribute the heat. If you have a solid-fuel cooker the manufacturer of your cooker will also supply you with special saucepans for cooking on the stove.

Looking after your pans

Cleanliness is of vital importance in the kitchen. All pans should be carefully washed out after use and stains should be removed by scouring, if necessary, unless the pan is of the non-stick or enamel variety. Copper on the bottom of pans should be cleaned with a solution of mixed vinegar and salt or with a commercial copper cleaner. Wash non-stick pans in hot soapy water but avoid the use of abrasives. Scourers should also not be used on cast iron as they may lead to pitting.

Basic requirements

One – small (2-pint) saucepan for making sauces, heating milk and small quantities of food.
Two – 3-pint pans for cooking vegetables.
One – 5-pint pan for cooking vegetables, soups and stews etc.
One – extra large saucepan for boiling puddings, making stock and poaching fowl.
One – large heavy frying pan.
One – small omelette and pancake frying pan.

Additional pans

A fish kettle for poaching fish – a narrow, oblong pan with a serrated tray in the base made in varying sizes.

A double boiler – a saucepan with a second smaller pan which fits into it, for very slow, gentle cooking. (A basin put on top of saucepan can be used for the same purpose.)

A steamer – a saucepan with a holed base which fits into another saucepan. Used for steaming fish and vegetables. A wire basket set over a saucepan of water can be used instead.

A pressure cooker – cooking food under pressure cuts the cooking time by up to as much as two-thirds and a pressure cooker is invaluable for those with families.

Casseroles

Although stews and casseroles can be cooked in saucepans they really respond best to being cooked in a vessel which is a slow conductor of heat and which retains the heat well. Choose a casserole which is 'flame-proof' as well as heat-proof and made from cast iron or steel-coated vitreous enamel.

Casseroles can be used both on top or inside the stove and are made in many attractive designs. Quality pays off and a good casserole can be used to advantage for cooking, serving and even storing food in a refrigerator.

Other equipment

Bain marie A deep metal tin with handles used for the slow and even cooking of pâtés and terrines which are put into the tin and surrounded by hot water.

Baking sheets or trays Most modern stoves come equipped with baking sheets or trays which can be used as an extra shelf in your oven. If you have to buy one, choose a size that will fit your oven space and which is not likely to warp.

Baking tins In different sizes for baking patties, pies and tartlets. Wash and wipe out carefully after using.

Bowls Also called basins. You will need a set of bowls in all sizes for storage, mixing and steaming. Some really pretty ones are now on sale and this is an area which it is well worth shopping around for bargains. To start off with have one large mixing bowl (over 4-pint capacity), at least two medium bowls and a small bowl for storing leftover sauces or meat dripping.

Boards Never use formica or other surfaces that can be scratched for cutting or chopping. Buy yourself a good-sized beech or elm wood chopping board and keep it within easy reach of your working surface. A marble or slate slab will prove an excellent aid in making pastry.

Baster For all roast dishes a baster (a rubber ball on the end of a plastic syringe) is both inexpensive and invaluable.

Brushes A pastry brush is a 'must' as you will use it for brushing pastries and pies with milk or beaten egg, greasing small tins and for brushing other ingredients with melted butter.

Colander A colander is a 'must' in the kitchen; a simple metal bowl on a slight stem, punched with holes and used for straining cooked vegetables and, in place of a steamer, for steaming vegetables and fish.

Deep-fat fryer Hot fat or vegetable oil tends to spit and even to boil over when raw ingredients are added to it and a deep layer of fat or oil is required for ingredients that call for being 'deep fried'.

A special saucepan is usually used for this purpose and supplied with a fitted, wire-mesh basket to make lifting out the fried ingredients more effective.

Electrical mixers, liquidisers and food processors etc. There are many electrical gadgets on sale which can help cut down time and increase efficiency in the kitchen. These are obviously optional extras for your basic kitchen equipment but electric mixers, liquidisers and food processors can cut hours from your time in the kitchen and be a real boon for the busy housewife. Look carefully at the machines on sale and buy one that is tough, easy to clean and well established – some machines are so complicated to set up and to wash up that in the long run it is almost quicker to do the job yourself. Check on the service facilities for the machine and that it has a good guarantee.

Fish slice Not only used for fish but for all frying; a flat metal implement with holes so that food can be lifted out and drained of excess fat.

Foil Kitchen foil (keep at least a couple of rolls) has many uses in the kitchen. Use it to line roasting pans to prevent them from getting so dirty; use foil for cooking foods that need to be really well sealed and for wrapping foods that are to be kept in the refrigerator.

Food mills One of the best gadgets ever invented for the kitchen and well worth-while buying since they are very reasonable in price. The food mill has three discs which grind against each other and can be used to strain or purée food.

Fruit juice squeezer For use with citrus fruit and the only successful way to extract the maximum juice from half an orange, lemon or grapefruit. The most simple versions can be as successful as the most expensive electrical squeezers, so pick your machine to suit your pocket.

Frying pans Weight and quality are vitally important for the success of your future cooking in the frying field so don't be seduced by inexpensive, lightweight and often non-stick pans. Choose a large heavy pan with a smooth surface, wash and dry it carefully before using the first time and wipe it out with some kitchen paper dipped in a little vegetable oil each time you use it to prevent sticking.

As well as a large basic frying pan for cooking anything from breakfasts to steak and a small pan to keep especially for making omelettes and pancakes, it is useful to have at least one non stick pan. For the best results the inside of the pan should be wiped out carefully with a soft cloth or kitchen paper each time you use it and not be washed. Care should be taken not to scratch the inside of the pan in any way.

Graters There are a good many stainless steel, metal and plastic graters on the market for grating cheese, vegetables and other ingredients; many include openings for slicing and different sides for coarse and fine gratings. Go for quality and strength rather than gimmicks – a grater is a functional piece of equipment and it is more important for it to work well than for it to look beautiful. A good, stainless steel grater may seem expensive but it should last you most of your life and save you money in the long run. Aim for a grater with areas for fine and coarse grating, rasping and slicing.

Hachoire A useful double-handled, double-knived chopper with curved blades for chopping herbs and vegetables.

Jugs Heat resistant glass measuring jugs are ideal for measuring all liquids and 'cup' quantities. Buy both a 2-pint and a 1-pint jug.

Kettle Buy a larger kettle than you think you need and you will not regret it. Most manufacturers of cookers will advise you on the best kettle to buy for their stove and, if you decide on an electric one, buy a model with a self switch off mechanism which operates as soon as the kettle boils as this makes for both economy and safety.

Kitchen paper Invaluable for draining fatty foods and for mopping and wiping. Fix up a holder near the sink.

Knives A collection of good sharp knives will help you to work more efficently and produce better results. Buy really top quality knives and a really good knife sharpener to keep them in tip-top condition. Sharpen your knives regularly once a week or even more often if you use them a lot and keep them separately from other kitchen equipment if you can – knives can be blunted just by jangling against other implements in a drawer. You will certainly need:

1. A carving knife with a large blade and easily gripped handle for carving roasts.
2. A small neat knife for peeling fruit and vegetables and chopping small items.
3. A small and large chopping knife; choose stout, slightly stubby knives for easy handling.

Mincing machine This is one of the kitchen utensils that comes into its own when meat stretching or using leftovers becomes a necessity to make the household budget accounts make sense. Best of all for this purpose is an electric food processor which finely chops rather than minces the meat but there are also good meat mincers on the market and here again the maxim is to buy the best.

Non-stick pans These are fine for light use, e.g. scrambled egg and will, I imagine, go on improving in quality and durability. If you buy non-stick pans of any kind never be tempted to scour them out to clean them, to use harsh abrasives or to stir or mix with any metal ended implement.

Pie dishes Although you can use casserole or fireproof glass dishes as a pie dish it is really worth while having one special pie dish which has a flattened edge on which you can secure your pie crust. Also invest in a crust support for pastry, a layered funnel which will support the top of your crust during the cooking time and prevent it from sinking into the filling ingredients.

Pressure cookers Although these are on the expensive side they are a great aid to cutting fuel costs when long slow cooking is required. Since they cook food under pressure in a hermetically sealed vessel which allows no steam to escape, all flavours and juices are retained in the food, and dishes are produced in about a third of the time they would take under normal circumstances.

Roasting tins Like baking sheets these are usually provided with your stove. Again it is worth-while buying an extra tin when you buy your stove.

Rolling pin You can choose between a cheap and tough wooden rolling pin and a more fragile glass pin which can be filled with iced water to help keep your pastry at the all-important cool temperature.

Rotary beater An efficient hand beater for beating or whisking liquids. Not necessary if you have an electric mixer.

Saucepans One of your major and most important outlays in the kitchen. Do buy the best and although I am afraid this often works out to be the most expensive it will also, in the long run, pay dividends. Good heavy saucepans with thick flat bottoms will cook evenly and burn less easily than the cheaper thinner ones and, like a good stove, they should last you a lifetime. Buy a set of saucepans that will fit into one another to save storage space.

Have a large double-handled pan for making stocks, boiling joints of meat or poultry, and for making stews and steaming puddings. Two smaller saucepans will be needed for puddings and one or two mini pans are essential for making sauces, boiling and poaching eggs and cooking small quanities of food.

Scales When you begin to cook you will want to measure quantities accurately although as you get more proficient you will find you can guess the weight of a good many ingredients with surprising accuracy. Buy scales that show both English and metric weights and which go up to at least 5 lb (2·5 kg).
Scissors Buy yourself a pair of good all-purpose scissors; you will find them invaluable for cutting tough joints of game and poultry, trimming fish, chopping parsley and a hundred and one other kitchen chores.
Sieves Sieves are an all important part of good cooking. Buy the best and get three sizes – a large coarse sieve, a fine hair sieve and a small strainer.
Slow cook casseroles Fairly new arrivals on the kitchen scene, these electrically operated stewing pots cook food at a very low heat over a long period using very little electricity. Casseroles and stews can be left to cook overnight or through the day and this kind of equipment can be a great boon to the working housewife who may like to prepare a dish first thing in the morning and leave it to cook by itself during the day.
Spatulas Have a wooden spatula for use with non-stick pans and omelette pans. A metal spatula is ideal for turning many fried foods. A plastic spatula is the best implement for scraping out bowls.
Spoons You cannot have too many spoons in a kitchen. To begin with you will need three wooden spoons of varying sizes, a large perforated metal spoon, one small and one large ladle for soups and sauces and a set of measuring spoons which will give you exact teaspoon, dessertspoon and tablespoon measurements.

Storage containers Another item that you cannot have too many of in the kitchen. Attractive jars, tins and boxes can be bought for storing anything from cakes to dried beans; used with imagination they can both provide useful storage space and also help to enliven your kitchen *décor.*

Tin opener Always an invaluable item. A wall opener is somewhat pricey but is always there whenever you want it; inexpensive openers tend to distort within quite a short time.

Vegetable peelers Far better at doing the job than you are. A good vegetable peeler is an economy and helps make a neat job of an often boring chore.

Whisk A small wire whisk costs next to nothing and yet can perform magic in the way of mixing sauces, salad dressings and even whisking ingredients.

It would take a whole book to describe the other cooking aids you can choose from to make life easier and more convenient in the kitchen. Now you can buy electric frying pans, infra-red grills, egg boilers and deep fat fryers to mention only a few. Most of them have their good points but before investing in one, and some of them are quite expensive, decide if you are really going to use them, whether you need them and whether you are going to get good value for your money. A machine specially for making toasted sandwiches may seem attractive but how often do you really want toasted sandwiches which could anyway be made without too much trouble under your grill? Items like these can be a waste of money if you are not careful and they take up space which may be at a premium.

Basic Cooking Methods

Whether you have an elaborate kitchen with every possible gadget it can contain or a small kitchenette with the simplest possible equipment, the basic cooking methods remain the same. Of course there are modern innovations such as infra-red grills and radiant cookers but in the long run cookery still amounts to the basic principles of cooking over heat, under heat or in an enclosed compartment where heat affects a cooking container from all sides.

Boiling

Cooking over a high heat so that the liquid is highly agitated and bubbles break through the surface. Although probably the simplest method of cooking, this is also one that can be grossly abused. Although one talks about boiled beef, fowl or fish these ingredients in fact have to be simmered or poached in their liquid, i.e. cooked at a lower temperature than that of boiling point; if they were boiled the flesh would be tough and lose its flavour.

Vegetables, pasta and eggs are boiled. Boiling point has to be reached in order to make syrups. Sauces are brought to boiling point and cooked over a high heat in order to reduce them and strengthen the flavour. Stocks are boiled; boiling point should be reached at some point when cooking leftover food in order to kill off any bacteria and 'boiling' is the term used when referring to sweet or savoury puddings which are cooked in a basin in or over boiling water.

Simmering

Cooking over a medium low heat so that the liquid is gently agitated but does not break into bubbles. Simmering is mainly used for the long, steady cooking of soups, stews, casseroles and boiled meats. Ingredients which are boiled instead of being simmered tend to become tough. In some cases it is difficult to obtain a flame that is low enough for simmering and if that is the case an asbestos mat for the purpose should be put over the heat.

Poaching

Still slower cooking than simmering with the water barely moving. This is a gentle process and usually used for delicate foods such as chicken breasts, fish and eggs.

Poaching can also be done in the oven as well as on top of the stove and the term *bain marie* is applied when ingredients such as custards are cooked in moulds placed in a pan of hot water in the oven.

Ingredients to be poached are usually put into warm or hot liquid and the heat is then lowered to slow simmering.

Steaming

Food set over boiling water and cooked in the steam that arises rather than by direct contact with hot liquid.

Steaming can be done by placing ingredients in a colander or sieve, balancing the colander or sieve over a saucepan containing a few inches of fast boiling water and then covering with a lid. This method, however, is not very satisfactory as much of the steam will probably escape and the whole point of steaming is that it ensures most of the flavour of the ingredients will be retained. If you want to steam food it is worth while investing in a steamer – a saucepan with a perforated base which will fit snugly into a slightly larger saucepan and come no more than half way down it.

Many vegetables respond well to steaming, and so do delicate foods such as white chicken meat and fish.

Cooking in a double boiler

One of the most gentle of all cooking methods, where food is cooked in a bowl or small pan set over hot, not boiling, water so that direct heat does not come into contact with the food.

Many sauces and egg custards will curdle if they are exposed to direct heat; cooking in a double boiler prevents this. You can use an ordinary kitchen bowl which fits into a saucepan suspending the bowl a few inches above the hot water or you can buy special double boilers for the purpose.

The container should never be allowed to come into contact with the water but always be above it.

Shallow-frying

Cooking food over a high heat in hot fat or oil.

The amount of fat or oil used for cooking depends on the individual recipe. Some frying is done in very little fat using only an ounce or two of butter, lard or dripping or a tablespoon or two of oil. Other dishes require enough fat to come half way up the ingredients to be cooked.

A heavy, flat bottomed and stable frying pan should be used.

The fat or oil for frying should always be heated to the correct temperature before the food is added. Frying should always be done in *hot* fat and the best way of testing the temperature before starting is to drop in a small piece of bread. If the fat is ready the bread should immediately sizzle and become golden brown.

Ingredients that are to be fried should always be well dried before being added to hot fat or oil.

Adding ingredients to hot fat or oil lowers the temperature so it is important not to attempt to fry too many ingredients at one time. Ingredients to be shallow-fried should be turned half way through the cooking time with a spatula; they should not be pierced with a sharp object.

After frying, drain on kitchen paper to remove excess fat in order that the ingredients may retain their crispness.

The fat can be strained through a hair sieve or through muslin and kept in a refrigerator for further use, with fat or oil that has been used for frying fish carefully labelled and not used for other ingredients.

Butter will burn if brought to too high a temperature. To prevent this add some vegetable oil to the butter.

Dripping must be clarified (see page 166) before being used.

Sautéing

This is merely another word for frying, although this particular term usually applies to food which is cooked in butter or a mixture of butter and oil in a frying pan over a medium to high heat.

Deep-fat frying

Food that is plunged into very hot fat or oil and cooked as quickly as possible on all sides.

Do not fill the pan that is to be used more than half full with fat or oil.

Heat the fat or oil up to the correct temperature before adding the ingredients and never try to add too many ingredients at one time.

If a large quantity of ingredients are to be used it is worth placing them in a basket before adding them to the hot fat or oil. It is possible to buy special pans, equipped with baskets for frying, but the pan in any case should always be large and heavy.

The fat or oil you use for deep frying should always be clean and free from sediment, and care should be taken to ensure that no water or other liquid, with the exception of made batters, is allowed into the hot fat or oil.

Most ingredients that are to be deep-fried need a coating of some kind (i.e. batter, flour, egg and breadcrumbs) and the crisp results should be drained on kitchen paper to remove excess fat before being served. Once some of the ingredients have been cooked the fat or oil should be allowed to re-heat before adding the next batch. Cooked, fried ingredients can be kept warm in a moderate oven and if necessary can be re-crisped by dropping them back into the hot fat or oil for a few seconds or by putting them into a hot oven for a minute or two.

Fat used to be the most popular ingredient for deep-fat frying but this has now been replaced by cooking oils of varying kinds which are cleaner and somewhat easier to handle, and also quicker to heat. Many oils on the market are guaranteed not to hold cooking odours but I still prefer to keep oil used for fish separate from that used for other ingredients. Oils vary in flavour and in price; my own favourite is sunflower oil but this is really a matter of personal taste.

The advantages of deep-fat frying are that it is a quick method of cooking food, gives an appetising crispness to ingredients and, in the case of batters, can produce a wide variety of inexpensive dishes. The disadvantages are that it has to be done at the last minute or the food will go flabby and that it fills the kitchen with strong odours which quickly turn stale and cling to the room.

Note: Shallow- and deep-fat frying are two of the most dangerous cooking procedures. Wet ingredients will sizzle and spit if added to hot fat or oil; if too many ingredients are added to hot fat or oil it is possible that the fat will foam over the top of the pan and could ignite.

Roasting

The original definition of the word 'roasting' was applied to ingredients that were cooked over or in front of an open wood fire. In these days the nearest we get to this method of cooking is by using a *rotiserie* over a barbecue in the garden and present day methods of cooking meat or poultry in an oven should more correctly be called 'baking'. Basting, or pouring fat over the ingredients while they are cooking, gives the crisp illusion of roasting.

Basting, except in the case of very fat joints of meat, is essential when roasting in order to prevent the meat drying out. Normally fat is laid on top of the joint to be roasted and, once it has melted, the fat together with the juices in the pan are scooped up and poured over the joint at about fifteen-minute intervals. If you do a lot of roasting a baster which consists of a rubber ball on the end of a plastic syringe is an inexpensive and useful piece of kitchen equipment.

Ingredients that are to be roasted nearly always require to be 'sealed' as the initial step of the cooking time. Meat is sealed by being put into a *hot* or *very hot* oven for a short period before the temperature of the oven is lowered. The sealing process ensures that the juices of the ingredient to be roasted are contained so that the joint will retain its moisture.

Roasting is a relatively quick method of cooking and therefore it should only be used for the better cuts of meat or top quality poultry and it is a waste of both time and money to try and adapt this method of cooking to pieces of meat only suited to stewing or casseroling.

Seasoning meat that is to be roasted is important but remember that salt rubbed into meat before it is roasted will tend to draw out the juices of the meat during the cooking time. Salt should be added towards the end of the cooking time.

Meat that is to be roasted can be 'marinated' (see page 5) before being cooked to give extra flavour and to help tenderise the flesh. It can also be larded (see page 5) to add extra moisture to the meat, stuffed (see page 8) to add flavour and bulk or have small slivers of garlic and other ingredients inserted into small pockets cut in the flesh of the joint to give an extra savoury taste.

Getting to know your Ingredients

Cooking is a science and when you cook you are dealing with fresh produce not inanimate objects. To cook well you have to get the feel of these ingredients, be able to differentiate between good and bad quality, recognise the texture of the produce and how you can use it to your best advantage. Cooking is a sensitive thing and much of it is done by feel and by tasting as you go along; too much cooking and you can ruin a potentially acceptable dish, too little and the food can be inedible.

Much of your cooking success will come by practice, a practice that will continue all your life as you get swifter and more adept at preparing and cooking food for your family and friends. Success will also come too if you know how to choose the right ingredients, how they will marry best together and by starting with the best quality available. Don't settle for second best; it is far better to make a simple stew from inexpensive meat than it is to try and produce a roast joint from a cut that has not the quality, texture or the flavour to be suited to that particular method of cooking and it is better by far to have no vegetables at all than to serve up produce that has been sitting around for too long, has gone limp, lost its flavour and, indeed, even developed an unpleasant sour taste.

Shopping for fresh produce

I find Tuesdays and Fridays the best days of the week for buying fresh meat, fish, poultry and vegetables. On those mornings most shops and markets seem to get their deliveries, you should be sure of getting produce that is really fresh and of having a good selection from which to choose. Mondays are always a particularly bad shopping day since most shops have only what has been left over from the weekend and the new fresh produce hasn't yet arrived; butchers are nearly always closed on Monday afternoon and fishmongers are usually closed throughout that day.

Prices of all fresh commodities vary in the most amazing way from one shop or source to another and the most expensive is by no means always the best. Take into account travel costs when you find a source of relatively inexpensive produce; by the time you have paid bus fares or car park tariffs you may not be saving much after all and might just as well spend a little more by shopping around the corner and save yourself time and money in the long run.

Storing fresh produce

Eggs
Store eggs in the least cold part of a refrigerator and allow them to warm to room temperature before using them.

Dairy foods
Cheese, except for cream or cottage cheese, should not be stored in the refrigerator as it tends to dry out, harden and impart its odour to other ingredients; cover cheese lightly and keep it in a cool dark place. In hot weather wrap cheese in a piece of muslin, slightly damped with a solution of one part vinegar to five parts water. Milk and yoghurt should always be kept in a refrigerator or in the coolest place possible and so should cream of any kind. Butter should also be stored in a refrigerator, if possible in a sealed container as it is extremely susceptible to absorbing other odours; leave butter that is to be used for spreading at room temperature for half an hour before using.

Meat
Unwrap meat as soon as you get it home, place it on a clean plate and put it into a refrigerator as quickly as possible.

Poultry
Unwrap poultry and remove the giblets from the cavity and wipe the inside of the bird with a damp cloth as soon as you can. Keep fresh poultry in a refrigerator.

Fish
Unwrap fish as soon as possible, wipe it with a damp cloth and store it in a refrigerator. Fish that has not been gutted should be cleaned as soon as possible and all fish should be cooked within twenty-four hours of purchasing.

Vegetables
Store root vegetables in a cool dark place; do not wash before storing. Use new potatoes as quickly as possible after they have been bought. Green vegetables should be packed in polythene bags and stored in the bottom of a refrigerator or a very cool dark place. (Some refrigerators have a compartment especially for storing vegetables.)

Salads
Salad stuff needs to be kept cool in order to retain its freshness and crisp quality. Clean and dry salad ingredients before wrapping loosely in a polythene bag or sealed container and store in the bottom of a refrigerator or a very cool dark place.

Fruit
Store fruit in a cool dark place removing any damaged or blemished fruit before storing. If melons are to be chilled in a refrigerator they should be sealed in a polythene bag as the smell will be absorbed by other refrigerated ingredients.

Bread, cake, pastry and biscuits
Store bread and cakes in a sealed airtight container. Pastry and biscuits should be stored in separate airtight containers – if pastry or biscuits are stored with bread or cakes they will lose their crispness.

Sausages, bacon and other commercial meat products
Store sausages and other commercial meat products, cooked or uncooked, lightly wrapped in the refrigerator and use as soon as possible.

Deep frozen foods
Deep frozen foods should be kept in the refrigerator and used within the period specified on the outside of the package.

Seasonings

Salt

Salt is necessary for almost all savoury foods but it should not be added with too heavy a hand. You can always add more salt at the table but it is difficult to subdue the taste once it has been added.

Coarse salt, rock or sea salt This is more expensive than ordinary table salt and is usually served at the table.

Plain salt or table salt The salt most usually used in cooking. Add salt to vegetables when they are cooking to help keep their colour and bring out their flavour. Add salt to almost all savoury dishes as they are cooking and test the flavour of the dish before serving to ascertain whther the flavouring and seasoning is strong enough.

Iodised salt More expensive than plain table salt but good for those who are on a diet. For those on a salt-free diet it is also possible to find salt substitutes in chemists.

Seasoned salt There are a number of seasoned salts on the market now and the taste of these can be very attractive and can help to add flavour to dishes that might otherwise be rather uninteresting. Seasoned salts to look out for are:

Garlic salt, celery salt, onion salt, mushroom salt and various mixed seasonings that include Italian seasoning, lamb seasoning, chicken seasoning, salad seasoning and steak seasoning etc.

Pepper

The choice of peppers on the market now is far wider than it used to be. The pepper comes from a vine that is grown in the Far East. Pepper should be used with a light hand; its slightly hot sensation helps to bring out the flavour of other ingredients. Green or unripe peppercorns can be bought in tins and have a delicious mild flavour.

Red peppercorns in jars, packed in brine, are now available and have a slightly stronger flavour than the green peppercorns; they have a most attractive appearance and go well with beef dishes.

Black pepper I would always recommend that the pepper mainly used in cookery (with the exception of white sauces and lightly coloured foods) should be black peppercorns, freshly ground at home through a peppermill. The flavour of freshly ground pepper is highly preferable to that of ready ground black pepper or of white pepper.

White pepper White pepper is made from black peppercorns

which have had their skins rubbed off and the flavour therefore is not nearly as strong as that of black peppercorns and does not have the robust, aromatic, lingering taste of freshly ground black pepper. White pepper, commercially or home ground, should, however, be used to season dishes that are of a light colour where specks of black would offend the eye.
Cayenne pepper A red pepper made from ground red chillies that is very hot indeed but a delicious savoury if used sparingly. Cayenne pepper goes particularly well with cheese dishes, fish and poultry.
Paprika pepper Another hot red pepper that should be used with care. Paprika has a very distinctive flavour and gives a very definite flavour to a dish.

Mustard
English mustard English mustard comes in dried or made up form and has a sharp, hot and pleasing taste that goes well in some casseroles and stews, with roast beef, ham and tongue, in some sauces and with cheese.
Other mustards There are so many rare and wonderful mustards available now that it would be impossible to try and describe them all. The alternative to English mustard that I use most in cooking is the French Dijon mustard that has a pleasant bright yellow colouring and a delicate flavour that goes well with cooked foods.

Vinegars
Malt vinegar This is a harsh, very strong vinegar and apart from sprinkling it over fish and chips, using it for pickling or chutney making and for making some traditional sauces such as mint sauce it is not really suitable for cooking. The wine vinegars or flavoured vinegars available from delicatessen shops have a much more delicate flavour.
Cider vinegar Less expensive than the wine vinegars, it is also extremely good for cooking.

Vinegars are used in salad sauces and for marinating meats, fish and poultry. The action of the acid in a vinegar helps to tenderise meats.

Bottled flavourings
Tomato ketchup Bottled ketchup is sometimes used to add flavour to a dish or a sauce but on the whole as its flavour is so distinctive, and tends to be rather vinegary, it is better to add

tomato flavouring with a home-made tomato sauce or with a tomato purée.
Tabasco sauce A very hot sauce that is made from chilli peppers. It adds a fiery flavour to dishes and goes well in soups and some sauces but it should be used sparingly.
Worcestershire sauce A strong brown sauce with a real bite to it. A few drops added to a soup, stews or casserole can lift a dish that is not very exciting to taste.
Anchovy essence Although anchovies are fish this sauce is used to give pep to meat and poultry as well as fish dishes and a few drops will be sufficient to give an interesting flavour to some soups, stews, casseroles and sauces.

Herbs

The use of herbs in cookery as a flavouring ingredient is almost as old as cooking itself and their subtle aromas have the most magical effect on a wide variety of dishes. Most commonly used herbs can be grown in this country on the kitchen windowsill or in the garden and, whenever possible, it is infinitely preferable to use the fresh rather than dried herbs which lose a lot of their flavour in the drying process. The nearest thing to fresh herbs are herbs that have been 'freeze dried' and seem to retain far more of their colour and scent than most dried herbs.

Use herbs sparingly as their flavour can be strong and it should not be allowed to swamp the taste of other ingredients. Chop them very finely before adding them to dishes and, if you have to use dried herbs, soak them in a little lemon juice for five minutes or so to allow them to develop their flavour and soften.

To chop parsley or other green herbs, remove the stalks, put the leaves in a mug and chop with kitchen scissors until the herbs are very finely cut.
Balm A herb with a lemony flavour; add it to salads or cold summer drinks, chicken casseroles or fish dishes.
Basil A classic Mediterranean herb that goes beautifully with all tomato dishes and salads.
Bay leaves An essential ingredient in stock making, and one or two leaves greatly improve the flavour of almost any stew or casserole. Bay leaves are also used to flavour milk for white sauces, custards and puddings, they should always be added to the liquid in which

fish is to be poached and they frequently appear as a garnish for the tops of pâtés and terrines.

Borage Used to decorate cool summer drinks.

Caraway Used to flavour madeira-style cakes and in spiced dishes, especially spiced red cabbage.

Chervil A very easily grown plant that is somewhat similar to parsley but with a much more distinctive flavour. Used in sauces to go with chicken, fish or eggs. A few very finely chopped leaves make a good garnish for a tomato soup, the flavour goes well with potato salads and the chopped herbs can be added to salad dressings.

Chives Grasslike spring onions with a strong onion flavouring. The finely chopped leaves make an excellent garnish for almost any cold dish; they are delicious in salads, mixed with cream cheese or with sour cream to serve with baked jacket potatoes.

Dill Rather an underrated herb in the UK although it is very widely used in Scandinavian cooking. Here again the flavour is very strong and the herb should be used sparingly. Both the seeds and the feathery leaves of this plant are used and the taste goes particularly well with all fish, and especially salmon dishes. Finely chopped dill leaves can also be added to potato salads, to the water in which new potatoes are cooked. They can also be used as a stuffing for almost any sea or river fish.

Fennel Sweet fennel is very similar to dill and can be used for the same purpose. Florentine fennel has edible bulbous stems that are crisp and white and can be eaten as a vegetable in their own right. The sliced stems can be used as a stuffing for fish.

Garlic One of the most widely used of all herbs with a strongly distinctive flavour that, if it is used correctly, can greatly enhance the flavour of most other ingredients.

Rub a cut clove of garlic around a salad bowl to give flavour to a summer salad. Serve garlic butter with French bread or as a garnish to steaks, hamburgers and fish. Rub joints of beef, pork or lamb with garlic before roasting them or insert small slivers of garlic into little pockets cut in the meat with a small, sharp pointed knife. Garlic goes well with all tomato dishes and is essential in a great many sauces and other dishes. Peel the garlic cloves before using and, when crushed garlic is required, crush the cloves with the back of a fork or through a garlic press.

Marjoram Sweet marjoram is a delightful old-fashioned herb. Finely chop the leaves to add to salads, sauces, soups and egg dishes. Cook some marjoram in stews and casseroles and use it in a *bouquet garni* for flavouring stocks and soup bases.

Mint There are a surprisingly wide number of mint variations which will grow easily in the garden; spearmint, apple mint, pineapple mint, peppermint and pennyroyal. Add to cheese and lamb dishes, egg dishes, omelettes and a wide variety of other dishes where a little extra flavouring is required.

Oregano A wild marjoram which is a must for tomato, lamb and most Italian meat dishes.

Parsley Probably the most widely used herb in England. Use it lavishly, very finely chopped, as an attractive green garnish to give a professional finish to a dish, give flavour to your stocks by adding the stalks and serve it very crisply fried as an accompaniment to fried fish.

Rosemary A strongly aromatic herb that is usually associated with the cooking of pork, lamb or chicken dishes. A few sprigs placed under a joint of pork, lamb or a chicken give the meat a wonderful flavour.

Sage Another strongly flavoured herb which can easily be overdone. Sage is used in a great many pork dishes and as a flavouring for sausages or for stuffings. Sage also goes well with cheese and onion dishes.

Summer savory Another herb that is often overlooked but was once very widely used in this country. The flavour goes well with almost any meat or poultry dish and, traditionally, a sprig of savory should be added to the water in which broad beans are cooked or finely chopped to add to a white sauce in which the beans are to be served.

Tarragon One of the loveliest of all herb flavourings. It goes particularly well with chicken. (One of my favourite summer dishes is chicken with a lemon and tarragon mayonnaise.)

Tarragon also goes well with cold summer soups and in other cold dishes.

Thyme Like sage, thyme has a most distinctive flavour and should be used sparingly. Use in savoury stuffings, in *bouquets garnis*, casseroles and stews.

Spices

Most spices have a very strong flavour and should be used very sparingly. Their flavour also develops during the cooking time so adjust the taste of a dish at the end rather than at the beginning of the cooking time.

Allspice Usually bought ground but also available in berries. Allspice, as its name suggests, seems to have the flavour of a great many spices all combined together. Use sparingly in some stews and casseroles and for some sweet, spiced dishes.

Cinnamon A delicious spice that is much used in the cooking of apple dishes.

Cloves Used in milk infusions for making sauces and for some pork and bacon dishes. Cloves are stuck into the skin of gammon when it is to be baked. Cloves are also traditionally incorporated into a good many apple dishes and are used in pickling.

Coriander Coriander can be grown out of doors in the UK and the leaves, finely chopped, are delicious in salads and other cold dishes. The ground seeds have a strong aromatic flavour and go well with tomato dishes.

Cummin Usually incorporated in curry dishes but the flavour also goes well with fish and egg dishes.

Ginger Root ginger can be bought fresh in many places now and has a quite different flavouring to the dried root. Ground ginger root is used in some highly spiced meat and poultry dishes, is served with melon and used in baking.

Juniper berries Soft berries that have the smell of pine forests about them. Juniper berries go well with game and with red meats and are often incorporated into pâtés.

Mace One of the great spices of the Far East. A little ground mace can work miracles with some meat dishes, with potted meats and fish and in pâtés.

Nutmeg Another of the great spices of the world. Add grated nutmeg to puréed vegetables as well as to a great many savoury dishes and sauces. Nutmeg is also used in many sweet dishes and has a delicate, haunting flavour.

Saffron One of the most expensive spices because the flavour comes from the tiny stamens of crocuses and these still have to be picked by hand. This bright orange spice colours everything it is added too as well as giving out a delicious smell and flavour. Saffron is widely used in Spanish cooking and is often added to cakes and some sweet dishes.

Turmeric One of the spices which gives curry its flavour. A yellow-coloured spice with a strong flavour that is very attractive.

Stocking your Larder

Providing you have the space (a large, cool, dark and dry cupboard will do) it makes good sense to keep a well-stocked larder of non-perishable food. The amount you keep depends on your space but remember that prices rise all the time and keeping a well-stocked larder can help cut down your weekly shopping time and also mean that you have ample supplies to cope with any emergency, a sudden influx of guests, times when you may be too busy to spend much time shopping or even times of illness. Buying dry goods in bulk will also help to save you money although it may require a considerable outlay in the first place.

Consider these questions before investing in a well-stocked larder:

Will you use the goods?
Have you got plenty of space to store them?
Can they be stored in suitable conditions?
Will you use them before they deteriorate?

Baking powder Used for making cakes and buns etc. Keep firmly sealed.

Bottled goods Vinegar, olive, soya, sunflower or mixed vegetable oil are amongst the essential ingredients used in the kitchen. Keep both malt and wine vinegar (red or white); olive oil, soya bean oil, sunflower oil or a mixture of olive and other vegetable oils are used for making salad dressings and for frying. For deep frying use a corn oil which is less expensive. Bovril or Marmite can be used for sandwiches and for adding flavour to sauces, soups and stews and keep a jar of both English and French Dijon mustard to use in salad dressings, some sauces and stews. You may also find it useful to have tomato ketchup, Worcester sauce, Tabasco sauce, a bottle of anchovy essence, mushroom ketchup and soy sauce at hand. Also available in bottles or jars are commercially made mayonnaise, grated horseradish and capers.

In the sweet line, raspberry jam and apricot jam are frequently used in pudding recipes; redcurrant jelly is a 'must' with lamb dishes and so is mint jelly or sauce.

Breadcrumbs Home made breadcrumbs can be kept in a sealed screw-topped jar. Packaged breadcrumbs are useful for emergencies.

Cereals Porridge, oats, barley, breakfast cereals etc. Store cereals in a dry place and, if they are to be kept for any length of time, transfer them to a sealed polythene container or a screw topped jar. Crisp up softened cereals in a medium hot oven for a few minutes. Porridge oats can be used as a coating for fish; crushed breakfast cornflakes can be used in the place of breadcrumbs or as a topping for a fish pie and pearl barley helps to stretch meat stews and soups.

Chocolate or cocoa powder Plain cooking chocolate is the best to use for cooking but plain cocoa powder can be used in its place if necessary. Keep tins of cocoa powder very firmly closed.

Coffee There are so many blends of coffee on the market that the only way to find out which one you really like best is to experiment with different blends and brands. You can buy your own roasted coffee beans and grind them yourself as you require them but the flavour of the roasted coffee will quickly deteriorate so you should buy roasted coffee beans in small quantities only. The contents of ground, instant coffee bought in bulk should be transferred to small airtight containers as soon as the package or tin is opened.

Dried and crystallised fruit A good selection of dried and crystallised fruit is invaluable to keep in your store cupboard for cake-making and for puddings. They keep well provided they are stored in a cool, dark and dry place.

Dried currants, sultanas and raisins are used for cake-making and for adding to steamed and other puddings.

Glacé cherries are used for cake-making and for decoration.

Angelica is used for the decoration of cold puddings.

Dates are added to cakes and to some breads and puddings.

Dried apple and pear slices can be soaked in water and then stewed for use in puddings.

Dried apricots and plums are used in both savoury and sweet dishes and need soaking before being used (they can also be cooked in a pressure cooker without having been soaked beforehand).

Dried milk It is always useful to have a supply of dried milk in your store cupboard. There are two varieties – dried milk or milk substitute which is used in dry form to sprinkle on top of tea or coffee, or dried milk or milk substitute which can be reconstituted to be used for cooking in the place of milk. Once opened the packets or tins will need to be thoroughly sealed again.

Dried vegetables Freeze dried vegetables and dried 'instant' potatoes are useful to have in your store cupboard. The vegetables can be added to soups, stews and casseroles to give extra body and flavour and 'instant' potato can be used as the basis of some made up dishes or as a pie topping.

Flour There are various kinds of flour and it is important to use the right kind for the job.

Plain white flour Used for sauces and thickening, for bread products and for some lighter pastry products, batters, fritters and pancakes.

Self-raising flour Used for some cake-making, puddings and some pastry products.

Strong white flour Flour made especially for bread-making strong flour has a high proportion of gluten and is ideal for plain breads.

Wholemeal flour The flour used for making brown breads.

Other flours There are many other flours (stone ground, wholemeal, farmhouse, rye, granary etc.) which are sold in health food stores and which are for making brown breads. These shops will usually supply you with leaflets on bread-making using these special flours.

Storing flour Flour must be stored in a dry place which should also be airy and cool. If the flour is kept in a container the container should be washed and carefully dried before new flour is put into it. Kept carefully, plain flour should keep for up to one year and self-raising flour for up to six months without deterioration.

Cooking with flour Many books recommend that you should sift flour before using it but today most flours are pre-sifted before being packaged. Unless the flour is old or damp it is not usually necessary to sift it before use.

Breads Most breads are made with yeast and require kneading to incorporate the flour into the other ingredients and to make a smooth, elastic, dough.

Cakes The flour added to cake mixture usually needs to be 'lightly folded into the other ingredients'; the best way to do this is to add one-third of the flour at a time and to fold it with light airy movements into the basic ingredients using a spoon or fork and figure-of-eight movements to that the flour is gently incorporated without being beaten in.

Thickening Stews and casseroles are often thickened by the addition of flour. The main ingredients (meat, chicken etc.) can be rolled in flour before being fried or a thickening liaison of flour and softened butter can be added to the stew or casserole during the last stage of cooking: mix one tablespoon flour with ½ oz butter until smooth liaison is formed. Add the liaison to the stew or casserole and stir over a medium heat until the sauce has thickened and is smooth and shining.

Gravies Flour is used to thicken gravies made from the juices in a roasting pan after the meat has been removed (see page 45). After the fat has been poured off the juices in the pan, the flour is added and stirred over a medium heat until it has browned (this is important in order to give the gravy a good colour) and then liquid is added to make the gravy. It is important to simmer the gravy for at least five minutes before serving it to allow the flour to cook and lose its slightly grainy, raw flavour.

Sauces Flour forms the thickening ingredients of many sauces. Usually butter is melted, the flour is added to the butter and stirred until the flour and butter forms a ball and comes away from the sides of the pan, then liquid is added to make the sauce. It is important to cook the sauce for at least 5 minutes after the addition of the liquid in order to allow the flour to cook and lose its slightly grainy, raw flavour.

Pastry With most pastry the flour is put with the salt into a bowl and then fat, cut into small pieces, is rubbed into it. At the end of this process the fat should have become the size of coarse breadcrumbs with the flour adhering to it.

Cornflour This is a very fine flour made from maize used for thickening some sauces and especially the sauces for Chinese cooking. The cornflour should always be mixed to a smooth paste with some liquid before being added to a sauce. When cornflour is first stirred into a sauce it has a cloudy appearance and the sauce should be stirred until this cloudiness disappears and the sauce is clear and glossy. Cornflour can also be added to plain flour to make extra light sponge cakes.

Food colourings Edible food colourings can help to improve the colour of some dishes. Green food colouring for instance is useful for adding to hot and cold spinach, lettuce and pea soups which may look rather insipid, and the red food colouring is useful to give richness to some puddings. Use food colourings extremely sparingly – a drop or two will always be quite adequate for your requirements.

Gelatine Gelatine is widely used in puddings and cold savoury dishes. The easiest way to buy it is in package form (each package contains enough gelatine to set 1 pint of liquid). Gelatine will keep indefinitely.

Herbs Herbs not only help to add flavour to dishes but they also give that little extra touch of professionalism which can make all the difference to a special meal. Although fresh or frozen herbs are the best for flavour there are some good commercial brands of dried and freeze-dried herbs on the market (one to look for is the Schwartz range). Add herbs to soups, stews, casseroles and egg dishes and, if you want to increase their flavour, soak them in a little lemon juice or warm water to help bring out their taste before using them. There are also some combinations of herbs and seasonings for special dishes (lamb seasoning, chicken seasoning etc.) which are very good indeed.

Nuts Nuts are expensive most of the year and the best time to buy them (providing you don't mind cracking the shells) is before Christmas when they are in season. Keep a supply of blanched almonds for using in sweet and savoury dishes (flaked or 'nibbed' almonds can be heated in a hot oven until golden brown and crisp and used as an attractive topping for sweet dishes).

Walnuts are used in cakes and some savoury dishes but they don't keep all that well once they have been shelled so these are definitely better for being stored in their shells – they are not difficult to shell and can be shelled as required.

Hazel-nuts are another useful ingredient to use for sweets and cakes and again they are best stored in their shells.

Pasta A variety of pasta in your larder can provide a large number of quick, inexpensive and exciting meals. Don't confine yourself to the more conventional types of pasta only. There are delicious variations made with eggs and all kinds of shapes and sizes each of which have their own texture and attraction. Cooked hot pasta can be dressed with any number of simple or more exotic sauces to make first or main courses and it also makes an extremely good basis for cold, summer salads. Keep pasta in a cool dry place and, once a package has been opened, store the remainder in an airtight container. 4 oz of pasta should be ample for each serving.

Spaghetti Can be bought in a variety of thicknesses and lengths and can be served plain with melted butter and grated Parmesan cheese or combined with a tomato or meat sauce, as well as a wide variety of other ingredients.

Macaroni Also comes in different thicknesses and is a hollow, tubular pasta. Use in the same way as spaghetti or incorporate with a rich cheese sauce to make a delicious macaroni cheese.

Canneloni Giant, tubular pasta which is cooked and then stuffed with a savoury filling and covered with a sauce.

Lasagne Flat sheets of pasta which are cooked and then layered with a savoury sauce and topped with a rich white sauce.

Pasta shapes Shells and bow shapes in different sizes which can be cooked in soup, added to stews, served with butter as a vegetable in the place of potatoes or served with a sauce as a main dish. These are particularly good with a vinaigrette or mayonnaise dressing, serve cold, as part of a salad menu.

Taglitelli or noodles Flat, narrow or wide pasta which cooks in minutes and is often enriched with eggs. There is a green variety flavoured with spinach. Taglitelli is served in the same way as spaghetti.

Pulses Dried peas, beans and lentils make inexpensive but nourishing additions to winter meals. The pulses can be used in soups or incorporated into stews or casseroles; they need to be soaked in cold water overnight and are usually boiled until soft before being added to a dish (the water the beans were soaked and cooked in should be used as it contains some of the goodness of the pulses).

Keep a stock of lentils (for soups and stews); red kidney beans (for making Chilli con Carne and for adding to stews and salad dishes); split green and yellow peas for making nourishing winter soups and butter beans for adding to stews and casseroles.

Salts and peppers There are various kinds of salt available and although you will obviously want some ordinary household salt in your kitchen you may also like to have a small supply of coarse sea salt to have on the table for special occasions.

Good cooks keep both white pepper and coarsely ground black pepper (preferably bought as whole peppercorns and ground when required in a pepper mill) handy; white pepper is used for those dishes in which flecks of black would be unattractive and the black pepper, which has a much better flavour, is used for everything else.

Suet, packaged Although fresh suet which you can buy from a butcher is far better and more strongly flavoured than that bought in a package it does not keep well. Packaged suet has a long shelf-life and it is useful to keep in your store cupboard for making sweet and savoury suet puddings.

Tinned and convenience packaged goods Tinned goods, despite popular belief, do not have an unlimited shelf-life and it is positively dangerous to use a tin that is damaged or swollen. Tins are also more expensive than using fresh food and their flavour (except with a few exceptions) is inferior. In my own larder I keep a stock of tinned tomatoes, tinned tuna fish, anchovies, butter beans and red kidney beans for adding to salads and for adding bulk to stretch casseroles, tinned consommé for using as the base for quick hot or cold soups and some mushrooms for using in quick snacks. I also keep baked beans for the children.

Store tinned food in a dark cool place and, wherever you can, buy it in bulk as you can make considerable savings this way. I must admit to not being a great advocate of convenience packaged foods. For one thing I find them expensive (the real thing is usually a lot cheaper) and for another I really do argue with many of the claims that they save time; in my experience by the time you have soaked, re-constituted and heated through the ingredients (not to mention reading the sometimes confusing instructions) you would not have taken very much longer if you had madc the real thing from scratch. As in everything, however, there are exceptions: stock cubes are available in this day and age; choose the best quality, buy them in bulk when you can and store them in a dry place. Packaged soups can make a quick and nourishing snack or starter especially if you add some of your own fresh ingredients.

Powdered custard is a must if you have children in the house, and if you add a little cream to the milk when making up the powder the flavour can be very good indeed.

Tubes of flavouring ingredients Tomato purée is best bought in tubes as, since one only uses a small quantity at a time, it keeps better and is easy to measure. English mustard can also be bought in tubes and I also find it useful to have a tube of cream cheese in the larder.

Yeast Dried yeast comes in small packages and keeps indefinitely providing the packages are not opened.

Storage chart for cooked and prepared foods and leftovers

Cooked meat	leave in one piece cover lightly	centre of refrigerator or cool larder	2–3 days
Cooked poultry	cover lightly	centre of refrigerator or cool larder	2–3 days
Cooked game	cover lightly	centre of refrigerator or cool larder	2–3 days
Cooked fish	cover lightly	near the top of the refrigerator	1–2 days
Cooked vegetables	cover lightly or keep in a polythene box	bottom of refrigerator or cool larder	3–5 days
Stocks and soups:			
meat	cover with foil	bottom of refrigerator	4–5 days
vegetable	cover with foil	bottom of refrigerator	2–3 days
Cooked casseroles, stews etc.	cover with foil	centre of refrigerator or cool larder	2–4 days
Milk puddings, custards etc.	cover with foil	bottom of refrigerator or cool larder	2–3 days
Cooked fruit, jellies etc.	cover lightly	bottom of refrigerator or cool larder	3–4 days

Storage chart for cooked and prepared foods and leftovers contd.

Raw fruit salads etc.	cover lightly	bottom of refrigerator or cool larder	3–4 days
Grated cheese	tightly covered container	refrigerator or dry cool place	10–14 days
Eggs:			
whites	covered container	refrigerator	4–5 days
yolks	covered with water to prevent hardening	refrigerator	3–5 days
Breadcrumbs:			
soft	tightly covered container	cool dry place	4–8 days
dried	tightly covered container	cool dry place	indefinitely
Pancakes	lightly covered	refrigerator or cool place	4–8 days
Raw pastry	well wrapped	bottom of refrigerator or cool larder	2–3 days

Meat

As meat is the most expensive item that you are liable to buy on your housekeeping budget, and as it will form a major ingredient of many of your main meals, it is important that shopping for meat should be done wisely and well. You will need to decide how much meat you need, what kind of dish you want to make, then choose the right kind of meat for that purpose and know how to cook it to the best possible advantage. It is an extravagance, for instance, to stew a top quality cut of meat which is better suited to roasting. Equally it is a mistake to try to treat a piece of stewing meat as though it were a roast.

It often pays to shop around before making your purchase. In my experience the price of different joints can vary considerably within a small area as butchers and supermarkets often have special offers; if you have a deep freeze, valuable savings can be made by buying meat in bulk when it is at its least expensive. You should also know how to recognise raw meat that will cook well and, when it comes to the table, will have both flavour and a good texture. Bargain buys are not always a hundred per cent reliable; the meat may have been badly frozen and lost blood on thawing, it may not have been hung long enough and the meat may not have been good quality to start with.

Often your most reliable source for buying top quality meat is a small family butcher who, once you get to know him and he realises you are going to be a regular customer, will advise you on the best value for money and make sure you are satisfied.

Storing meat

Meat should be unwrapped as soon as you get it home and never stored in the wrapping it was brought in. Store meat in a refrigerator and, if you do re-wrap it, do so lightly so that air can circulate around the meat. Large cuts of beef can be stored in the top of a refrigerator for as long as a week but smaller cuts, mince and pork should be eaten as soon as possible.

Cooked meat should be wrapped before being stored in the refrigerator to prevent it drying and leftover cooked meat dishes should be allowed to cool and then be covered before refrigerating. Cooked foods can be hazardous and should be eaten as soon as possible; they should always be brought to boiling point if they are to be re-heated to prevent any chance of bacteria.

Roasting meat

There are two ways of roasting meat – for a top quality joint the best method is in a hot oven at 425°F/220°C Reg 7; the heat sears the skin on the outside sealing in the flavour; meat that may be slightly more tough is usually roasted in a moderately hot oven (375°F/190°C Reg 5) for a longer period so that there is less shrinkage in the joint and the meat has more time to become tender.

The meat should be put in a roasting pan, in the centre of a preheated oven with the fatty side of the meat upwards. If the meat is very lean more fat or some oil should be added. The meat should be regularly basted throughout the cooking time. To give it an extra crisp coating the joint can be sprinkled with a little seasoned flour before the last fifteen minutes of cooking time.

Roasting in foil or roasting bags

This method can be used for the second quality roasting joints because sealing the meat in a roasting bag or foil helps to tenderise the meat. The foil parcel or bag should be opened up for the last 30 minutes of cooking time to give the meat colour which it would otherwise lack.

Grilling meat

Trim off any excess fat from the meat (some fat should remain to prevent the meat becoming too dry but it is best to remove any fat in excess of about ½ inch).

Season the meat with pepper but do not add salt which will draw out the moisture from the meat – salt can be added when the meat is partially or wholly cooked.

Brush the meat with melted butter or cooking oil and cook it under a medium hot grill turning it once or twice during the cooking time and basting the meat with the juices which drip into the pan.

Frying meat

Like grilling, frying is an extremely quick method of cooking and is only suitable for the more expensive, small cuts of meat like steaks, cutlets, chops and some offal. If cheaper cuts of meat are used they will remain tough as frying will not allow them the time to become tenderised. Little fat should be used in cooking and the pan should be heated before the meat is added. The meat is usually cooked over a very high heat.

Trim the meat, cutting off any fat in excess of ½ inch to prevent the meat drying as it cooks. Before cooking season the meat with pepper, but not with salt which draws out the moisture leaving the meat dry. Brush a large heavy frying pan with a thin film of melted butter or cooking oil, add the meat and cook it over a high heat to brown and seal both sides. Lower the heat to medium and continue to cook until the meat is tender. Season with salt before serving.

Accompaniments for grilled and fried meats
Lemon is a natural partner to grilled and fried meats which may be on the fatty side – lemon juice helps to break down the fat so serve with quarters of lemon as a garnish. Quarters of tomato and sprigs of fresh parsley also make attractive garnishes for grilled and fried meats.

Steaks can be served with a savoury butter. Butter is flavoured with finely chopped parsley or other herbs, garlic or mustard and the butter is served in thin slices placed on top of the meat just before it is to be served.

Boiling meat

Silverside or brisket of beef and leg of lamb can all be simmered, after being brought to the boil, with vegetables and herbs to make excellent dishes.

Pot roasting meat

A compromise can be reached between roasting and braising meat by cooking joints, which are not of the quality of roasting joints, in a covered pot. The meat is quickly browned in a pan or in a very hot oven and then transferred to a covered pan and cooked with some stock and a good variety of vegetables.

Braising meat

For this method of cooking, the rougher joints of meat are cooked in a tightly covered pan in the oven with the joint being placed on top of a bed of chopped vegetables. The top of the pan is removed for the last 30 minutes of cooking time to allow the meat to brown.

Stewing or casseroling meat

One of the most popular ways of cooking the less expensive cuts of meat. After being tossed in flour the meat is quickly browned in a little hot fat or oil and is then put into a heavy casserole with vegetables and stock or other liquid. The casserole is tightly covered and the dish cooked slowly on top of the stove or in a moderate or low oven until it is absolutely tender. The cooking time varies according to the quality of the meat.

Stews and casseroles should be rich combinations of meat, vegetables and flavourings. Onions, carrots, celery, turnip and fresh herbs all help to give flavour. The liquid can be supplied by stock, water and stock cubes, tomato juice or tinned tomatoes or a mixture of stock and wine or cider.

Season stews and casseroles with salt and pepper and add a small amount of spice (ground mace, nutmeg, allspice, cinnamon or ground cloves, or a combination of spices) together with a good bouquet of fresh or dried herbs. Extra flavour can be added to a stew by stirring in tomato purée, Worcestershire sauce, Harvey's sauce or mushroom ketchup. Stews can be thickened by adding a *roux* (a blend of softened butter and flour) just before serving.

Salt or pickled meat

Silverside or brisket of beef, some cuts of pork and ox tongue are sometimes sold salted or pickled. The meat will need to be soaked in cold water for up to four hours (or even overnight) to remove excess salt and it is then gently simmered until tender.

Carving meat

A well-carved joint can stretch twice as far as one that is literally hacked to pieces. Butchering is also important for the carving of an economical joint; a well-shaped and cut joint will be far easier to carve than a roughly shaped or cut piece of meat. Boned and rolled joints are easier to carve than meat on the bone.

A well-sharpened knife and a carving fork with a guard are essential tools for good economical carving. Make sure your knife is razor sharp (you may find it worth investing in an electric carving knife). Most joints are carved against the grain and the normal practice is to start at the thickest part of the joint. In order to allow the meat to settle and compact before carving it is good practice to leave the meat to stand in a warm place for 5 minutes before carving it and the meat should be served immediately it has been cut.

Making gravy for roast joints

The best gravy is made from the juices in the pan in which the joint was cooked as these juices contain a lot of flavour and goodness. As soon as the joint is cooked transfer it to a warmed serving dish and leave it to stand in a warm place or low oven for 5 minutes while you make the gravy.

Pour off excess fat from the roasting tin and place the tin with the juices from the joint over a low heat. Add 1 tablespoon flour and stir over the heat until the flour has become brown. Gradually stir in $\frac{3}{4}$ pint stock, water and a stock cube, or the water in which vegetables have been cooked, stirring all the time until the gravy comes to the boil and is thick and smooth (if the colour of the gravy is not dark enough you can add a little Bovril, Marmite, mushroom ketchup or gravy browning). Strain the gravy into a sauceboat through a fine sieve.

The quantities of meat you will require

The following quantities are a rough guide to the amount of meat you will need to allow for each serving. The quantites will obviously be altered by the amount of vegetables you add to a made up dish.

Meat for roasting
Meat that is on the bone. Allow 8–12 oz per serving.
Meat that is off the bone. Allow 6–8 oz per serving.

Meat for stewing or casseroling
Meat that is cooked on the bone. Allow 8–12 oz per serving.
Meat that is bought off the bone. Allow 6–8 oz per serving.

Meat for grilling or frying
Steaks. Allow 5–10 oz per serving.

Offal

Often the most delicate and delicious parts of an animal are surprisingly inexpensive to buy. For a long time there was such an abundance of meat which people could afford to buy that these off-cuts fell out of favour. Now, however, as meat prices rise and rise, offal is gradually coming back into its own and regaining the reputation it once had for making good, inexpensive and nourishing meals.

Calves' or lambs' brains
Brains must be absolutely fresh when they are bought and they do not really respond very well to freezing.

Soak the brains in cold water for 30 minutes, rinse under cold running water and drain well. Remove any blood arteries and place the brains in saucepan. Cover them with cold water, add a teaspoon of lemon juice and a little salt, bring gently to the oil and simmer for 5–10 minutes. Plunge the brains into cold water, drain well, chill and then slice for cooking.

Brains can be served in a cream sauce, fried in butter or used in pâtés; they can also be served cold in a vinaigrette sauce.

Calves' and lambs' sweetbreads
Sweetbreads are glands which come from the throat or close to the heart. Freshness is again of paramount importance when buying sweetbreads, which should look moist and plump. They make delicious and delicate eating and are prepared in the same way as brains. The sweetbreads can be parboiled in stock to give them extra flavour and after cooling should be pressed under a plate to remove all excess moisture. They can be used in the same way as brains.

Ox, calves', lambs' and pork tongues
Boiled tongue can be served hot or cold (pressed) and as it contains very little fat it makes for economical eating. Tongues should be soaked in cold water to which 1 tablespoon of vinegar or lemon juice has been added for one hour before boiling. Tongues are placed in a large heavy saucepan with onion, carrots, celery and a *bouquet garni*, covered with water, seasoned with salt and pepper, brought to the boil and simmered very gently until tender. The tongue is then removed from the water (the liquid can be used for stock), the skin is stripped off and the small bones from the root of the tongue are removed. The tongue can now be pressed or cut into slices and served with a sauce. Salted or pickled tongues should be thoroughly soaked overnight before being cooked.

Lambs' and calves' hearts
Hearts are a little rich for some people's taste and benefit from being stuffed with a savoury stuffing, or served with a savoury sauce. Hearts should be braised in a very moderate oven.

Calves', lambs' and pigs' liver
Ox liver tends to be a bit strong in flavour and calves', lambs' and pigs' livers are the varieties which appear most in the kitchen. Calves' and lambs' liver can be roasted whole or stuffed and roasted, or cut into very thin slices and stewed or fried. Pigs' liver is usually used for stewing or for making pâtés and terrines.

Liver can be soaked in milk before being used, to get rid of some of the very rich flavouring.

Ox, calves', lambs' and pigs' kidneys
All of these make delicious eating and you should not be put off by the slightly strong, rich smell they have as this can be overcome by proper cleaning and soaking. Ox, veal and pork kidneys are sliced before cooking and lambs' are usually halved.

Remove outer membrane from the kidneys with a sharp, pointed knife. Split ox and pork kidneys in half and remove the white core from the centre – the fat surrounding the kidneys is suet which can be shredded and used for puddings.

To get rid of the strong odour of ox and pork kidneys they should be soaked in cold water to which 1 tablespoon of vinegar or lemon juice has been added for one hour. Lambs' and calves' kidneys should not be soaked.

Ox and pork kidneys can be parboiled in boiling water for one minute before being cooked.

Kidneys are usually fried, sautéed, grilled or added to pies.

Tripe

Although the lining of the stomach does not sound very attractive, tripe can be delicious and is very digestible. Tripe is bought dressed from a butcher (prepared for cooking by a lengthy process of soaking and boiling); there are two types, flat and honeycomb, of which honeycomb is inclined to be the most tender. Tripe is usually parboiled and cut into strips before being cooked. It can be grilled, fried, incorporated into a soup or cooked in a stew.

Ox tail

Although ox tail requires long slow stewing it has a delicious flavour and contains a good deal of nourishment. You will need about 3 lb of ox tail for 4–6 servings and you should ask the butcher to cut it into joints for you. The tail is stewed for soup or casseroles.

Pigs' trotters

Pigs' trotters make good eating in their own right and they also add strength and a gelatinous texture to stocks and casseroles. Remove any hairs from the feet by singeing them over an open flame. Soak the trotters in cold water for 1 hour before cooking. Trotters should be cooked slowly in water to which vegetables and a *bouquet garni* have been added; they can be split and served cold with a vinaigrette dressing or they can be split, egg and breadcrumbed and then fried.

Poultry offal

Chicken, turkey and duck livers are delicious cooked in many ways. They can be fried or grilled or used to make pâtés. Any green discolouration on the liver should be cut off before the livers are prepared for cooking. Poultry giblets can be used to make stock for soups, sauces or gravies and the gizzards and hearts can be used to make delicious stews, casseroles or pies.

The necks and feet of poultry can be added to stock to give both richness and flavour.

Lamb

English lamb is a meat that varies considerably according to the season and therefore the price of lamb fluctuates a great deal. Summer and autumn is the best time to buy lamb and it is usually at its most expensive in the early spring.

Imported lamb is usually available all the year round and tends to be marginally cheaper than the home-produced meat; it does however have less flavour than English lamb.

When you are buying lamb look for a good fresh colour (the younger the animal the paler the flesh will be). The meat of joints from a young animal should be pale clear pink with firm creamy or white fat. The meat from older animals (which will not be quite so tender but which has more flavour) should be a clear bright light red colour.

Avoid chops or liver of lamb which have a dull, dry or dark look to them.

Leg of lamb can be given extra flavour by inserting thin slivers of garlic into slits made through the skin of the joint.

Cold lamb is never all that popular so try to buy a joint which can be eaten when it is hot.

Cuts of lamb

Loin of lamb
A top quality joint which is sold whole, boned and rolled (usually cooked with a stuffing) or cut into chops. The whole or rolled joint is highly suitable for roasting and the chops are ideal for frying or grilling.

Leg of lamb
A quality joint that is primarily used for roasting. The leg can be boned, stuffed and rolled and the meat is also used for special stews and casseroles. Cubes of lamb from the leg can be used in kebabs and slices are sometimes cut from the thick end of the leg and are then fried as steaks.

Shoulder
The meat of a shoulder of lamb is comparable to that of the leg although it is more difficult to carve and has a higher percentage of bone to meat. The meat is usually roasted but it can be cut into cubes and used for stews and casseroles. Allow 12 oz of shoulder of lamb cooked on the bone for each serving. Shoulder of lamb is sometimes boned, stuffed and rolled.

Best end neck of lamb (also known as rack of lamb)
These are the delicate and delicious cutlets of lamb. The whole joint of cutlets responds well to being roasted: the joint should be trimmed (the top of the cutlets are cut off and the top ¾ inch of the bones trimmed); the joint can also be 'chined' (the ribs are severed close to the spine to make the joint easier to carve into cutlets). Cutlets should be trimmed and then grilled or fried. The boned and skinned meat from the whole best end neck of lamb (a cut similar to a fillet of beef) can be rolled and tied and then cut into thick steaks to be fried or grilled.

A guard of honour is an attractive joint made up from two best ends of neck of lamb (about seven cutlets in each) chined and interlaced with the fat side out and then roasted.

Crown roast of lamb is one of the most spectacular joints of all. It consists of two best end necks of lamb (seven cutlets each), chopped between the bones to about half-way through with the tops of the bones trimmed (the bones being bent around), and fat side out to form a crown. The centre of the crown is usually stuffed with savoury stuffing.

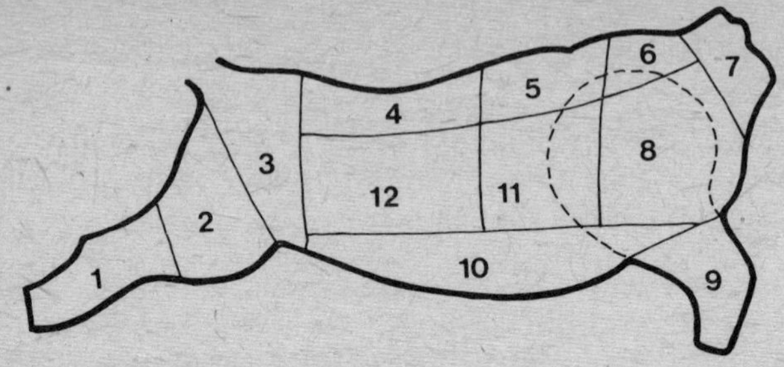

A Side of Lamb

1. Shank

1. and 2. Leg

3. Fillet

4. Loin chops or
4. and 12. Saddle (taken from a whole lamb)

5. Best end (used for Crown Roast and Guards of Honour)

6. Middle neck chops and cutlets

7. Scrag end of neck

6. and 8. Shoulder (off the bone for stewing)

9. Shank

10. Breast

11. Cutlets

12. and 4. Loin chops or saddle (taken from a whole lamb)

Dotted line – Whole shoulder of lamb

Chops
Chops can be grilled, fried, braised or stewed. They are cut from the loin and the best quality are the 'chump' chops from the end of the loin nearest the leg. 1–2 chops are allowed for each serving depending on their size. Excess fat is usually cut from the chops before they are cooked.

Cutlets of lamb
These are the tender thin chops from the best end of neck and they are excellent for grilling or frying. If the cutlets are small you will need to allow three cutlets for each serving. The top end of the bone is chopped off and the cutlets should be trimmed before being cooked.

Breast of lamb
Although this is a fat cut of lamb it does have a very good flavour and it is often very good value for money. The most popular way of cooking the breast is to bone and roll it with a filling of savoury stuffing but the joint can also be slow roasted and braised. A delicious way of cooking the breast is to simmer it in water until tender, remove the small bones, press the meat down firmly, leave it to get cold and then cut it into finger-thick slices; dip the slices in egg and seasoned breadcrumbs and then fry them until golden brown and crisp.

Middle and scrag end of lamb
The cheapest cuts of lamb that have a high proportion of fat and bone to meat but which are still full of flavour. The middle neck and scrag end are cut into pieces and cooked on the bone in a casserole or stew.

Accompaniments for lamb dishes
Roast lamb, cutlets and chops are usually served with a mint sauce or jelly and with redcurrant jelly. Boiled lamb or mutton is traditionally served with a well-flavoured onion or caper sauce.

Beef

Beef is the most expensive meat you are likely to buy and therefore care should be taken to ensure you have spent your money well. Good beef is hung for a week or more before being butchered and this not only helps to give the meat flavour but also helps to tenderise it.

The lean meat of beef should be bright red in colour and look bright and moist. The fat of the meat should be a good bright yellow colour and small flecks (or marbling) of fat through the lean meat will ensure you have a moist and succulent joint.

Avoid meat which has a dried appearance or which is dark and not bright red, cuts of beef which have a line of gristle in between the lean and fat meat and beef that is pale and pink in colour.

Meat sold on the bone is cheaper than meat cut from the bone and can often be good value; beef roasted on the bone tends to have more flavour than a boned joint but it is more difficult to carve. A butcher will often bone and roll the meat for you or, with practice, you can learn how to do this job yourself; the bones can be used to make stock.

Cuts of beef

Sirloin
A large top quality joint for roasting with tender, well-flavoured meat. The cut can include the fillet which is the most tender of all the cuts and the joint is sold on the bone or boned and rolled.

Rump
The joint next to the sirloin, rump is well flavcured and tender. The meat is usually sold in thick slices and is ideal for grilling or frying as steaks. A whole piece of rump can be roasted but is an extremely expensive joint and the cut can also be used for top quality made up dishes like steak and kidney puddings and *boeuf stroganoff*.

Fillet
Although fillet is the most tender of all cuts of beef it does not have the flavour of rump or sirloin. The meat is cut from the sirloin in a long, thick sausage-shape and can be roasted whole or cut either into thick 'tournedo' or the thinner *filet mignon* steaks and grilled or fried. *Châteaubriand* steak is cut from the centre, or eye, of the fillet and is usually roasted whole and then cut into thick slices.

Entrecôte
A cut from the ribs of beef which has a tender texture and a good flavour. The meat is either roasted in one piece or cut into thin steaks and fried or grilled.

Rib
Another large joint which also has good flavour but is not quite as tender as sirloin. The meat can be cooked on the bone or boned and rolled and the joint is suitable for roasting, braising or pot roasting.

Topside
Topside is sold off the bone and rolled. Although it has good flavour the leanness of the meat makes it inclined to be tough and the joint should be slow roasted, braised or pot roasted. Extra moisture can be added by larding the meat with small slivers of fat.

Brisket
Brisket is sold on or off the bone and consists of layers of fat and lean meat. The meat has a good flavour and is tender enough to be slow roasted although it responds best to braising or pot roasting.

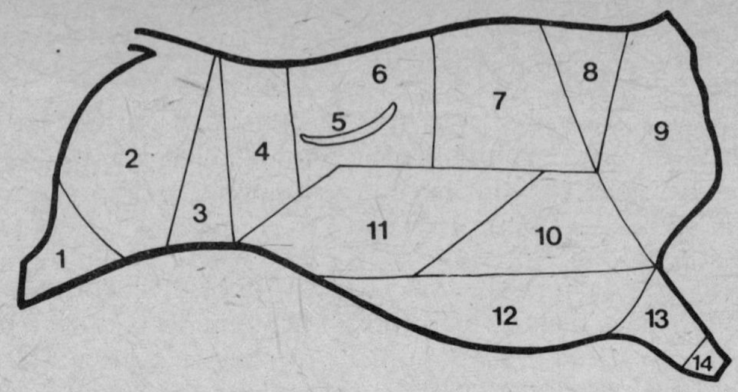

A Side of Beef

1. Shin
2. Round: round steak and topside; silverside and tail end of rump
3. Aitchbone
4. Tail end of rump; head of sirloin steak
5. Fillet steak
6. Baron including sirloin steak (head end)
7. Rib roast
8. Chuck steak
9. Neck
10. Shoulder
11. Short and rolled rib, flank and skirt
12. Brisket
13. Shin
14. Knuckle

Brisket responds well to salting and the salted meat makes an excellent boiled joint.

Silverside
A leaner joint than the brisket and one that is always sold off the bone. The meat is rather on the tough side and needs long slow cooking. It is suitable for braising or slow pot roasting. Silverside can be salted and makes a good lean joint for boiling, with vegetables.

Flank
Thick and thin flank comes from the belly of beef and is inclined to be tough and rather coarse. It is, however, excellent material for stewing and casseroling; providing the meat is very slowly cooked it can also be braised or pot roasted in a piece.

Skirt
Similar to flank – well flavoured and lean but on the tough side. Casserole, stew or use for pies and pasties.

Chuck or blade steak
Although called 'steak' chuck or blade are not suitable for grilling or frying and this can sometimes lead to some confusion. The meat is lean and of good texture and is suitable for stewing or casseroling.

Neck
Lean but tough meat – stew or casserole.

Leg and shin
Usually the cheapest of beef cuts and although they are tough and need a lot of cooking both leg and shin have a very good flavour. Use these cuts for stewing, casseroling and other slowly cooked dishes.

Minced beef
Disappointing results with dishes made from minced beef are often caused by the meat being of inferior quality – just because it is minced it doesn't mean that the meat will magically become tender when you cook it. Most dishes that require minced meat really need a good quality meat. It therefore pays to buy your meat and either mince it yourself or ask a butcher to do it for you. Buy chuck or blade steak for the best results and make sure there is a certain percentage of fat to the lean meat.

Beware of cheap offers of minced meat on sale. If they are cheap they are probably made up from tough scraps of meat left over from butchering.

Accompaniments to serve with beef

Yorkshire pudding is traditionally served with roast beef together with a choice of French or English mustard and horseradish sauce. Onion or caper sauce can be served with boiled salt beef.

Pork

Not so long ago pork was only sold during the colder weather as the meat does not keep well and can be dangerous if it is kept in a warm place. Modern methods of refrigeration have changed all that and the meat is on sale all the year round although it does fluctuate in price from month to month. Care should always be taken to keep pork cool (preferably in a refrigerator) and it should be cooked as soon as possible.

Colour and smell are both important when choosing your meat. The colour should be clear and bright pale pink. The meat should look moist and should smell sweet and fresh. Roasting joints should have a good layer of firm clear white fat and the skin should not be too thick.

To make carving easier, and to help crispen the outside of the joint, the skin should be scored through at ½ inch intervals – your butcher will usually do this for you.

To keep boned joints of pork moist, stuff them with a savoury sage and onion stuffing.

Cuts of pork

Leg of pork

A top quality joint which, since it is usually a large joint, is usually cut into two. The joint should be scored and it is either roasted on the bone or boned, stuffed and rolled.

Loin
Another quality joint but one that is inclined to be expensive and has a high percentage of bone to meat. The joint can be roasted whole or it can be boned, stuffed and rolled. The skin should be scored before roasting and the kidney (which is often attached to the joint) is normally left in when the joint is roasted whole.

Fillet
An extremely tender, sausage-shaped cut of meat. The fillet can be roasted or braised, or sliced, beaten and fried. As it is completely lean the fillet needs plenty of larding or moisture if it is to be roasted or braised – the fillet is often wrapped around with rashers of fat bacon.

Chops
Cut from the loin and delicious, they are a little on the fatty side. Chops can be grilled or fried.

Hand and spring
Joints for roasting cut from the foreleg of the animal. Hand and spring of pork can also be boned, cut into cubes and stewed or casseroled.

Blade bone of pork
Another joint which is usually roasted.

Belly of pork
Although this is a joint with a high percentage of fat it can make an excellent and cheap dish. The belly can be roasted or braised, or cut into thin slices and fried. Salt belly of pork is delicious boiled and served cold with baked potatoes, salad and pickles.

Spare rib of pork
The bones cut from the belly of pork with a small amount of flesh on them. The bones are separated and grilled or roasted with frequent bastings of a well-flavoured sauce.

Bath chap
This delicious speciality of the West Country has, sadly, become rather difficult to find. Cured pig's cheek is rolled in breadcrumbs making a very tasty and relatively inexpensive cold dish. The Bath chap is served cut into thin slices.

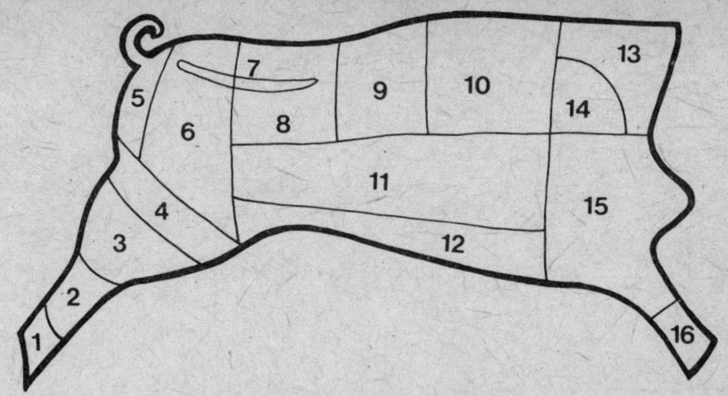

A Side of Pork

1. Trotter
2. Trotter
3. Knuckle or hock
4. Leg (gammon slices)
5. Slipper

5. and 6. Gammon

7. Fillet
8. Loin (hind), chump chops and loin chops
9. Fore loin and loin chops
10. Chine or shoulder cutlets
11. Streaky bacon
12. Belly
13. Spare rib
14. Blade bone
15. Hand
16. Pig's Trotter

Accompaniments for pork

The traditional accompaniment for roast pork is apple sauce. If the joint is not boned, stuffed and rolled, small balls of stuffing, fried or roasted with the meat, can be served with the joint and redcurrant jelly or fried slices of apple can replace the usual apple purée sauce.

Bacon

I find bacon (cured, or cured and smoked, cuts of pig) one of the most versatile and useful cooking ingredients for everyday cooking. Rashers of bacon, grilled or fried, can be served for almost any meal: they can be used as part of a main course or as a garnishing; boiled bacon or gammon makes a relatively inexpensive hot or cold dish; bacon rinds add flavour to stocks and chopped bacon gives a lift to almost any casserole, pie or stew. The flavour of bacon seems to marry up with almost any major ingredients be it meat, chicken or fish. Ham, by the way, as opposed to bacon is the thigh of a pig, removed and cured separately in a different way from bacon. See Ham, page 65. Bacon is cured by being immersed in a salt and water brine.

Green or fresh bacon Bacon that is cured but not smoked. This has a mild flavour and a white rind; the fat is white and the lean meat should be bright fresh pink in colour.

Smoked bacon Bacon that is cured and then smoked. It has a stronger and more salty flavour than fresh or green bacon and when it is used care should be taken not to over salt a dish in which smoked bacon is to be incorporated. Joints of smoked bacon which are to be boiled should usually be soaked before they are boiled – always check with your supplier who should be able to tell you how long the joint may need to be soaked before being cooked.

The choice between smoked and fresh or green bacon is a matter of personal choice.

Back bacon rashers These come in three cuts, 'prime', 'long' and 'top back' all of which have a high percentage of lean meat bordered by a thin strip of fat.

Wide and thin streaky bacon Cheaper than the back cuts and with the lean meat and fat mixed in strips – good for frying and grilling.

Middle or through cut rashers A mixture of streaky and back cut rashers.

Collar bacon rashers Wide lean rashers that are a little coarse for frying or grilling but perfect for using in made up dishes.
Gammon rashers Lean rashers with very little fat and a good flavour. These are usually cut thicker than back or streaky bacon and used for main course dishes rather than for breakfast or snack meals.
Oyster and flank rashers Rashers with a high percentage of fat which are used for larding meat and poultry to give flavour and to keep the ingredients moist.

Joints for boiling
Whole gammon A large joint weighing up to 14 lb.
Half gammon A large joint weighing 7–8 lb.

The joint can be cooked for 15 to 20 minutes less than the allotted time so that the rind can be removed and the fat covered with breadcrumbs (see page 63 for boiled and baked corner gammon).
Corner gammon A smaller joint of up to 4 lb with no bone. A neat joint for boiling which is easy to carve.
Gammon slipper Weight about 2 lb boneless and therefore easy to carve.
Gammon hock One of the cheapest of bacon joints which often includes some bone which is full of flavour and makes a delicious hot or cold dish.
Collar Another good bacon joint for boiling with a fair proportion of fat but, again, a good flavour.
Forehock and knuckle Slightly coarse texture but well flavoured and very suitable for soups and some bean and bacon combinations that require long slow cooking.

Preparing joint for boiling
If you buy bacon or gammon for boiling in a supermarket you may well find that it is vacuum packed in polythene or tied in a string vest all ready for boiling in its package or string bag. Instructions for the boiling time are usually included in the package. If you buy bacon for boiling from a butcher he will almost always tie the joint for you to prevent it falling apart during the cooking time. If the joint has a bone in it your butcher will almost always take this out and roll and tie the joint for you – ask for the bone which will add flavour to stocks.

Time for cooking boiled bacon
Smoked bacon joints should be soaked in cold water for three to

four hours, changing the water once or twice during that time. The bacon is then put into a saucepan, covered with cold water, brought to the boil and simmered for 20 minutes to each pound and 20 minutes over. If the joint is to be served cold, it can be left to cool in the water. The rind can be removed, the fat of the bacon dredged with breadcrumbs and the joint re-heated in a moderate oven (350°F/190°C Reg 4) until it is hot through. Serve the joint cold with salad or in a made up dish.

Unsmoked 'green' or 'fresh bacon' joints should be cooked in the same way but without being soaked first.

Baking bacon joints
If joints are to be baked rather than just boiled they need a preliminary boiling in order to tenderise them. Soak the joint if it is smoked and parboil for half the time. Remove the water, wrap in foil and bake for 25 minutes to the pound in a hot oven (375°F/190°C Reg 5).

Packaged bacon
Much of the bacon sold in this country is now vacuum packed in polythene. Packages show a date by which the bacon should be eaten and once the package has been opened the bacon should be removed from the polytheme and re-wrapped in greaseproof paper. Store bacon in the refrigerator either wrapped or in a sealed container as its smell is likely to be absorbed by other produce.

Fried bacon
Remove the rind with kitchen scissors and cut out any bones or gristle. Heat a frying pan over a medium high heat without extra fat. Add the bacon and cook over a medium low heat until the fat loses its transparency. Some people like their bacon crisp and others do not; the longer you cook it the crisper it will become. Reserve the bacon fat to use for cooking other ingredients.

Grill bacon
Line a grilling pan with foil. Replace the rack and place the bacon rashers (with the rind removed) on the rack. Cook fat bacon without extra fat, turning it frequently until the fat becomes transparent. Lean bacon should be brushed with a little melted butter or fat before being grilled.

Bacon rolls
Rolls of bacon make an attractive accompaniment to roast chicken

or they can be served with a mixed grill or fried liver. Use streaky bacon, remove the rinds and roll the rashers up tightly. The rolls can be placed around the chicken for the last 30 minutes of cooking time or they can be grilled separately.

Bacon as a garnishing
Finely chopped or cooked and crumbled bacon makes an excellent garnish for a great many dishes and soups. You can also add cooked chopped or crumbled bacon to salads to give crispness and a delicious flavour.

Either remove the rind from the bacon rashers and fry them until really crisp without using extra fat. Drain the cooked rashers on kitchen paper and leave to cool. Crumble the cold bacon into small pieces.

Or, remove the bacon rinds and cut the rashers into very small pieces before cooking. Fry the bacon without extra fat until the pieces are crisp, drain on kitchen paper and leave to cool.

Ham

Ham is produced from the top leg or thigh of a pig which is usually dry cured in a mixture of salt and saltpetre. Some hams are smoked after having been dry cured.

York ham Dry cured ham with a mild flavour and a somewhat pale colour. The ham should be well matured.

Brabenham A sweet cured ham with a black skin.

Virginia ham Sweet cured with a spiced and smoky flavour.

Parma ham An Italian speciality which is eaten raw. Some of the Italian Prosciutto are wind dried and others cured by a special process.

These days it is difficult for the housewife to cook a whole ham at home (you need large saucepans and the ham requires a long cooking process). Whole cooked hams can be bought for special occasions.

Serving ham
Cold ham, cut into slices, goes well with any salad dish or cold meat platter. Slices of ham can also be wrapped around tinned or cooked asparagus spears to make a pleasant summer dish. Mustard should always be served with ham.

Relatively small amounts of cooked ham are often incorporated into made up dishes or added to mixed salad dishes (see Ham and Rice Salad, page 150).

Hot or cold ham can be served with a Cumberland sauce.

Poultry

Chicken

Once chicken was a luxury food. Now, because of improved methods of poultry rearing, chicken has become an everyday part of our lives and is quickly replacing roast beef as a Sunday lunch-time dish.

The choice of chickens available can be confusing. Should you buy fresh or frozen chickens? What is the difference between a capon and a boiling fowl? How good a value are chicken portions?

Frozen chicken

Because birds can be reared to order and frozen as soon as they reach their prime, freezing has enabled poultry producers to produce relatively inexpensive birds for the table. Their taste may not be quite as good as that of a fresh bird but, providing they are treated with respect, frozen poultry can provide really good value for money.

Frozen chicken *must* be completely thawed before cooking and once thawed it should not be re-frozen unless the chicken has been thoroughly cooked. Ideally chicken should be thawed in the bottom of a refrigerator but, if you are in a hurry, it can be thawed at room temperature. Once a chicken has been thawed it should be cooked within 24 hours. A medium-sized chicken will require about 36 hours thawing time in a refrigerator and about 10 hours in room temperature. Chicken portions thaw much more quickly.

Fresh chickens
Fresh chickens are bought from a butcher or poulterer and tend to have a fuller flavour than frozen birds. They are sold ready for the oven. If you plan to buy and freeze fresh chickens make sure they really are fresh and have not been frozen and then thawed by the retailer.

Poussins
Small chickens usually split and grilled weighing about 1 lb.

Broiler chickens
Young chickens that are very tender and weigh around 2½ lb.

Capons
These are large birds weighing from 5–8 lb and good value for a party or special occasion. The birds should be cooked reasonably slowly so that they do not become tough.

Boiling fowl
Usually hens that have passed their laying prime and have good flavour but are inclined to be tough. Boiling fowl are less expensive than roasting birds and need to be boiled (poached), casseroled or slowly roasted.

Chicken portions
These can be grilled, fried, casseroled or stewed and are useful for meals that are quickly prepared. Chicken portions can be good value but one must remember that you miss out on the carcass of the bird which is invaluable for making stocks and on the giblets which provide wonderful flavouring.

Basic ways of cooking chicken

Roasting By stuffing a chicken you not only add flavour but also help to stretch the dish.

Roasting birds should be cooked in a hot oven (425°F/220°C Reg 7) for 15 minutes and then in a moderate oven (350°F/180°C Reg 4) for a further 1¼ hours or until tender. The bird should be basted frequently during the cooking time and should be covered by greaseproof paper or foil if it gets too brown.

Spit roasting If your oven has a spit roasting attachment this can

be a delicious way to roast a chicken. Allow about 1 hour roasting for a 3 lb bird, baste frequently and cook in a moderately hot heat.
Grilling Suitable for chicken portions. Brush the portions with melted butter or oil and cook about 4 inches from the heat for 20–30 minutes turning frequently.
Frying Fry chicken portions in hot fat or oil for about 15 minutes on each side.
Casseroling or stewing Cook chicken portions for about 40 minutes or a whole chicken for 30 minutes per pound.
Boiling Used for tough birds which should be poached rather than boiled because fast cooking will toughen the flesh. Cook over a low heat so that the liquid is just moving for about 40 minutes per pound. Old chicken can be steamed for 2 hours and then roasted to crisp the skin.
Using leftover chicken I once made eight dishes from a cooked chicken serving four people each time and there are endless exciting hot and cold dishes which will make good use of the remaining pieces of a cooked chicken. Small amounts of cooked chicken can be cubed and incorporated into salads; minced chicken can be made into rissoles and croquettes; cold chicken can be re-heated in a sauce, added to soups and used in a thousand different ways. A raw or even a cooked chicken carcass should never be thrown away; it will make an excellent stock and provide a good basis for soup, gravy or sauce (see Stocks page 68).

Jointing a chicken
It is never all that pleasant dealing with raw flesh but once you get used to jointing a chicken you will find it is a chore that can be done in no time at all.

Before cutting up the chicken, remove any fat from inside the carcass together with the giblets (neck, gizzard, heart and liver) which have been left inside the bird. Use a sharp knife and cut off the parson's nose (the tail), the end of the drumsticks if they have been left on (any scaly bits below the joints) and the tips of the wings – you can use a strong pair of kitchen scissors for this.

Quartering a chicken
Place the chicken on a chopping board and cut lengthwise through the breastbone (again a pair of strong kitchen scissors may help with this operation). Open the bird out and cut through the backbone. Cut each chicken half in half again diagonally between the wings and thighs.

Boning a chicken

Cut off the thighs and wings of the bird and, using a small sharp knife, cut off the flesh from the bones removing any sinews. Cut off the breast as close as possible to the bone and trim off any flesh from the underneath of the bird.

Carving a roast or boiled chicken

It is amazing how much difference there is between a good carver and a moderate one. A good carver can stretch a medium-sized chicken to five substantial portions and still have some over whereas a moderate carver will come up with enough for four and even that might look a little on the mean side. Always leave a chicken to 'rest' for five or ten minutes after it has been removed from the oven as this will consolidate the flesh and make the bird easier and more economical to carve. Use a really razor-sharp knife and sharpen if necessary half-way through carving. Kitchen scissors can be useful to help separate the joints.

Steady the chicken while carving with a carving fork. Insert the knife between the leg and body and cut through the thigh of the drumstick at the ball and socket joint. Cut the drumstick in two.

Remove the wing on the same side of the bird allowing a slice of breast to be included in the portion. Cut off the breast in thin slices from the front to the back of the bird.

Accompaniments to roast chicken

Roast chicken is served with gravy and sometimes with a bread sauce. It can be stuffed with a savoury stuffing and also served with chipolata sausages and bacon rolls which can be cooked alongside the bird.

How do you know when the chicken is cooked?

Chicken should always be served thoroughly cooked. One way to test it, and this is perfect for chicken portions and quarters, is to prod the flesh with a sharp fork at its thickest point. The fork should go easily through the flesh and the juice that runs out should be absolutely clear with no trace of blood.

If you prod a whole chicken in the same way some of the flavour is lost as the juice runs out, so a better way to test the bird is to pull gently at the leg of the chicken. If the chicken is tender the leg should pull easily from the breast and then spring back into place again.

Herby roast chicken

Chickens are not fatty birds and therefore they need to be cooked with extra moisture in order to keep them moist and also give that pleasant golden tinge to the skin. In this recipe a mixture of softened butter is spread between the chicken skin and breast meat giving the flesh a deliciously moist and flavoured taste. This does take a little time but the effort is well worth-while.

Serves 4–6

3½ lb chicken
4 oz softened butter
1 tablespoon finely chopped parsley
1 tablespoon finely chopped fresh thyme (or half teaspoon dried thyme)
1 teaspoon finely chopped rosemary
½ clove garlic
grated rind of 1 lemon
6 rashers streaky bacon
salt and freshly ground black pepper

Wipe the chicken with a damp cloth.

Combine the softened butter with the herbs and the garlic (peeled and pressed through a garlic press), season with salt and pepper, add the lemon rind and mix until smooth.

Using a small sharp knife, separate the chicken skin from the breast at the back of the bird, sliding the knife under the skin and taking care not to pierce it. Using your fingers, gently separate the skin from the breast flesh along the top and sides of the bird, easing your fingers gently forward. Place half the butter mixture in between the skin and the flesh and smooth it gently along the flesh. Spread the rest of the butter mixture over the outside of the bird over the breast, wings and legs. Place the bird in a roasting tin and cook in a pre-heated hot oven (400°F/200°C Reg 6) for 10 minutes and then lower the heat to moderate (350°F/180°C Reg 4) and continue to cook for a further 1–1¼ hours until the bird is tender, basting frequently with the juices that collect in the bottom of the pan.

Cook the rashers until crisp in a frying pan without using extra fat, arrange them on a heated serving dish and top with the chicken.

Note For additional flavouring, half a lemon or some sprigs of thyme, rosemary or tarragon may be placed inside the bird.

Roast stuffed chicken

Serves 4–6

$3\frac{1}{2}$ lb roasting chicken
2 oz bacon
3 tablespoons shredded beef suet
4 oz fresh white breadcrumbs
1 tablespoon finely chopped parsley
2 teaspoons mixed dried herbs
grated rind of $\frac{1}{2}$ lemon
1 egg
salt and pepper
chicken stock
2 oz softened butter

Mince the bacon rashers. Combine the bacon with the suet, breadcrumbs, parsley and herbs and mix well. Add the lemon rind, the egg beaten until smooth, salt and pepper and enough stock to bind the ingredients together.

Wipe the chicken and fill the stuffing into the cavity. Close the end of the bird with a skewer to keep in the stuffing as the bird cooks. Rub the softened butter all over the bird and season with salt and pepper.

Roast the bird in a hot oven (400°F/200°C Reg 6) for 10 minutes and then lower the heat to moderate (350°F/180°C Reg 4) and continue to cook for a further $1\frac{1}{4}$ hours or until the bird is tender. Baste frequently with the juices in the pan and cover the breast of the bird with greaseproof paper or foil if it begins to burn or dry out too much.

Remove the skewer and serve a spoonful of stuffing with each serving.

Boiled chicken with vegetables

Serves 6

3–$3\frac{1}{2}$ lb boiling fowl
water
2 stock cubes
2 parsley stalks
4 bay leaves
salt and freshly ground black pepper
$\frac{1}{2}$ lemon
2 large carrots
12 small onions or shallots

1 parsnip
1 large leek
$1\frac{1}{2}$ oz butter
2 tablespoons flour
$\frac{1}{2}$ pint chicken stock
juice of $\frac{1}{2}$ lemon
$\frac{1}{4}$ teaspoon mace
2 tablespoons finely chopped parsley
3 tablespoons double cream

Place the chicken in a large saucepan, add enough water to cover the bird, the bay leaves, parsley stalks, $\frac{1}{2}$ lemon, stock cubes and a little salt and pepper. Bring to the boil, skim off any scum from the surface, cover and simmer gently for $\frac{3}{4}$ hour. Remove the bay leaves, parsley stalks and lemon. Peel and chop the carrots and parsnip. Peel the onions and thickly slice the leek. Add the vegetables to the chicken, return to the boil and continue to simmer for a further 20–30 minutes until the vegetables and chicken are tender. Melt the butter in a saucepan, add the flour and mix well. Gradually blend in $\frac{1}{2}$ pint of the chicken stock, stirring continuously over a medium heat until the sauce is thick and smooth. Add the mace and lemon juice and mix well. Add the parsley and cream and heat through, stirring continuously until the sauce is hot but not boiling. Season with salt and pepper. Place the chicken in the centre of a heated serving dish, surround with the strained vegetables and serve the sauce separately.

Note Alternatively, the chicken can be carved before serving and arranged in the dish with the sauce poured over it. In this case, not all the chicken will need to be used and the remainder can go into a chicken soup.

Chicken and bacon rissoles

Serves 4
3 slices white bread
10 oz cooked chicken
4 oz mushrooms
6 oz bacon rashers with rinds removed
1 egg
2 teaspoons capers
pinch cayenne
beaten egg and breadcrumbs for coating
oil or lard for frying

Remove the crusts from the bread and grate the slices through a coarse grater. Mince the chicken with the mushrooms and bacon. Chop the capers very finely.

Combine the bread, chicken, mushrooms, bacon and capers, add the egg, season with a little cayenne pepper and mix well. Flour your hands and shape the mixture into thick sausage lengths about 2 inches long. Dip the rissoles into beaten egg and coat them in breadcrumbs.

Fry the rissoles in very hot lard or oil for about 8 minutes turning them frequently so that they become crisp and golden brown on the sides.

Golden roast chicken

Serves 4–6

3–3½ lb roasting chicken
¼ teaspoon cumin
¼ teaspoon turmeric
¼ teaspoon ground ginger
1 clove garlic
½ oz butter
1 tablespoon thick honey
1 teaspoon made English mustard
1 teaspoon finely grated lemon rind
salt and pepper

Wipe the chicken. Combine the cumin, turmeric, ginger and garlic in a mortar and pound to a paste with a pestle. Blend in the butter, honey, mustard and lemon rind and season with salt and pepper.

Rub the chicken all over with the mixture and wrap it lightly in tinfoil. Roast in a hot oven (400°F/200°C Reg 6) for about 1 hour until tender. Open up foil on the top for the last 10 minutes in order to give a golden crispness to the skin of the bird.

Turkey

Once only a feature of Christmas or perhaps bank holidays the turkey is now appearing more and more frequently on the table as modern methods of farming have made it possible to produce turkeys of a size more suitable for family meals. Turkey portions are also on sale in most supermarkets and make good eating. The turkey hen is better value than the cock because, weight for weight, the hen bird has a higher proportion of flesh to bones. The hen also tends to be more tender than the cock bird. When buying an oven ready bird allow ¾ lb weight per person for a small bird and ½–¾ lb per person for a large bird of over 20 lb.

Frozen turkey
Frozen turkey can be very good value but remember that you must allow at least 48 hours to thaw out the bird before you cook it. Cooking a half-frozen bird can be dangerous as bacteria is not killed and food poisoning may follow.

Roasting turkey
Turkey should be roasted by the slow method of roasting rather than by cooking them in a hot oven where it will tend to dry out. The bird will also need constant basting although this can be avoided by covering the whole of the bird with a muslin cloth well soaked in melted butter – the cloth is removed for the last half hour of cooking time. Stuffing not only helps to stretch the meat of the bird but it also helps to add flavour and moisture. Usually both ends of the turkey are stuffed, with different stuffing at each end (i.e. a chestnut stuffing at the neck end and a sage and onion or other savoury bread based stuffing at the other).

The breast of the turkey, being the thinnest part, tends to cook more quickly than the legs and (unless you use the muslin method) the breast should be protected by some foil or bacon rashers for most of the cooking time to prevent the breast drying.

Roasting chart for turkey
Roast the bird in a moderately low oven (325°F/165°C Reg 3).

10–12 lb	13–16 lb	17–20 lb
approx. 3½ hours	approx. 4 hours	approx. 5 hours

For the last 30 minutes of cooking time remove any covering from the breast, dust with flour, baste well and raise the heat to moderately hot (375°F/190°C Reg 5) to brown the skin. The bird is cooked when a fork plunged into the thigh joint produces a clear liquid and when the meat is shrinking from the end of the drumsticks.

Duck

Ducks have more bones and less flesh than chicken and pound for pound they work out to be more expensive. Ducks do, however, have a most delicious flavour and make a good celebration meal. Ducks also tend to be very fatty and this is something to watch when you are buying one; if the bird is overfat you will find that most of it disappears during the cooking time.

To minimise the richness of a duck remove any loose fat from the cavity and around the neck. Rub the inside of the bird with a cut lemon and stuff the bird with a savoury stuffing.

Ducks are trussed and roasted in very much the same way as chickens, but they will not need basting. The bird should, however, be turned two or three times during the cooking time.

Use only a young duck for roasting and cook it in the centre of a pre-heated moderate oven (350°F/180°C Reg 4) for 85–90 minutes (for a 4½ lb bird) allowing an extra 20 minutes if the bird is stuffed.

Older birds can be jointed in the same way as chicken and stewed or casseroled. Care must be taken to remove excess fat from the dish before it is served.

Rabbit

Rabbit is becoming a more and more popular form of food now that they are being farmed on a fairly extensive scale. The meat is not unlike that of chicken (firm white flesh) and has a good flavour. It can be used for all dishes that require chicken as their main ingredient.

When choosing a rabbit look for meat that smells really fresh, is plump with a good ratio of meat to bones and with flesh that is nice and moist. If the kidney of the rabbit has a good surrounding of fat it is a fair indication that the animal will be a good one. Rabbit tends to be a bit indigestible and it is worth while soaking the flesh in some vinegar and water (1 dessertspoon white wine vinegar to 2 pints water) overnight as this will help to tenderise and whiten the flesh. Rabbit can also be marinated in oil and lemon juice to give it extra flavour.

Jointing a rabbit

Cut off all the legs and the 'wings' from the ribs. Cut the back, or saddle, into three or four pieces.

Rabbit pieces can be grilled, stewed, casseroled or made into a pie or soup to provide nourishing and not too expensive meals.

Fish

There are over a hundred varieties of fish sold in our fishmongers and supermarkets so it is not surprising that people sometimes get a bit confused when they come to select the right fish for their particular requirements.

Eating fish makes good sense. There is little wastage and it requires only a short cooking time. It is rich in protein, fats, minerals and vitamins – especially vitamins B and D – as well as iron and iodine.

Choosing fish

Fish must be fresh. Stale fish is not only unpleasant to eat but smells bad and can actually be dangerous to eat. Don't be ashamed to bend down and sniff the fish on the fishmonger's slab; it should smell of the sea – a pleasant smell of ocean and fresh air. The eyes of all fish should be clear and bright and slightly protruding, scales should be bright and shining and never flaking from the skin. Gills should be red or pink and the flesh of the fish should be firm to the touch.

Shellfish is particularly dangerous unless it is absolutely fresh. Shellfish sold in the shell should always be tightly closed or should close if tapped; the shells of crab and lobster should be bright and firm and be heavy in proportion to the size. Prawns should be curled and not limp and the flesh of scallops should be clear and bright.

Smoked fish should be glossy with a freshly smoked smell.

Storing fish

Eat fish as soon as you can after it has been brought home. Unwrap it, sprinkle with a little salt if you intend to keep it overnight, wrap it lightly in some moisture-proof paper and keep it in the coldest part of the refrigerator, away from butter, cream and other items which easily absorb odours. If the fish is a whole one it is best to gut and clean it before storing.

Frozen fish bought in packets should be transferred to your own deep freeze as quickly as possible. If the fish is to be eaten rather than stored it should be used within 24 hours of purchase.

Preparing fish for cooking

Cleaning

Always wash fish as quickly as possible under *cold* running water. Do not clean fish in hot water or leave fish to soak.

To prepare a whole fish for cooking, place it on a table or counter top with a clean damp cloth under the fish to prevent it slipping about. Hold it firmly by the tail and, using a blunt stubby knife, scrape off the scales working from the tail to the head.

Using a sharp pointed knife, slit the fish down the length of its belly from the gills. Pull out the innards, clean away any blood and wipe the inside of the fish with a clean, damp cloth. Cut around the fins on the underside (kitchen scissors can be used for this) and cut out the gills. Unless the fish is to be served whole (in which case remove the eyes) neatly cut off the head and tail. Cut out the dorsal fin from the top of the back by cutting along each side and then pulling the fin firmly towards the head. Remove the fins from the underside in the same way. Wash the cleaned fish under cold running water and pat dry before using.

Filleting

Flat fish, i.e. sole, plaice, dabs etc. Flat fish are usually filleted into four half fillets, two from each side unless the fish are small.

Clean and scale the fish as above. Use a small but extremely sharp knife with a pointed end. Place the fish flat on a damp cloth on a table or working top. Cut a slit on either side of the backbone as close as you possibly can to the backbone and about $\frac{1}{4}$-inch deep on both sides. Working from head to tail slide the knife in through the cut you have already made, keep the knife as close as possible to the backbone and slide it from head to tail using long clean strokes, not a jabbing movement, so that the fillet comes cleanly away from one half side of the fish. Turn the fish round and cut off the second fillet, this time working from tail to head giving you two neat fillets. Fillet the other side of the fish in the same way.

Round fish, i.e. mackerel, bass, mullet etc. Herrings are usually split, the backbone being removed in one piece with the fish intact and merely flattened in appearance. Slit the herring right down the belly, clean and gently flatten out the fish. Working from the tail end, slide the knife under the backbone and gently ease it from the flesh of the fish.

To fillet round fish cut down the centre back of the fish to the bone from head to tail. Cut right along the belly of the fish. Work from the head down and slide the knife with short quick strokes keeping as close to the bone as possible. Turn over the fish and cut off the second fillet in the same way. The two fillets can be cut diagonally into two or three pieces if they are large.

Stuffing

Whole round fish Gut and clean the fish and place the stuffing in the belly cavity. Do not overstuff because the stuffing is likely to swell during the cooking time and may split the fish. Fasten together the sides of the belly with toothpicks which should be removed before serving.

Whole flat fish Using a small sharp pointed knife slit along the centre back of the fish on either side of the backbone making a pocket about 1-inch deep. Press the stuffing into the cavities on both sides and fasten the opening, if necessary, with toothpicks which should be removed before serving (the fish can be cooked in foil in which case the toothpicks are not really necessary).

Fillets of fish Spread a $\frac{1}{4}$-inch thick layer of stuffing on each fillet, roll them lightly and fasten them with a toothpick to keep their shape.

To sandwich two fillets Spread one fillet with about $\frac{1}{4}$ inch of stuffing, place a similarly shaped fillet on top and press lightly together.

Fish cutlets Wipe the cutlets with a damp cloth and neatly cut out the backbone. Press the stuffing into the cavity left by the backbone.

How much fish do you need for each serving?

When you look at an array of differently shaped and sized fish in your fishmonger's you may well find it difficult to know how much fish to buy for your family for the purpose for which you need it. The following ideas on the quantity of fish to buy will provide you with a rough guide.

Quantity of fish required for each serving
Whole fish Ungutted, to allow for cleaning and the removal of the head and tail etc., ¾–1 lb per serving:
Gutted, 10–14 oz per serving:
Oily fish ungutted (mackerel, herring etc.), 12 oz per serving:
Oily fish gutted, 10–12 oz per serving.
Fish fillets Lean white fish (cod, haddock etc.), 6 oz:
Oily fish, 5 oz.
Fish steaks Lean white fish, 7 oz:
Oily fish, 6 oz.
Salmon on the bone 8 oz per head if it is the tail; 5 oz per head if it is the middle cut.

Poaching

Fish should be poached very gently with the water only just moving.

Clean and prepare fish before poaching and cook it in water, seasoned with salt and pepper and with a *bouquet garni* added, water and wine, fish stock or a *court bouillon.* The cooking liquid can also be flavoured with some finely chopped shallots to give extra flavour.

Cover the fish with cold liquid, bring it gently to the boil, lower the heat until bubbles are only just breaking through the surface of the liquid, cover and cook gently until the flesh of the fish is just beginning to flake.

Fish to be poached should be of good quality; fish suitable for poaching are good quality fillets or steaks or white fish, trout, salmon and whiting.

Frying

Whole medium sized fish (i.e. herrings, mackerel, small grey mullet etc.) can be fried in a mixture of butter and oil. Fillets of fish are usually coated with egg and breadcrumbs before being fried and oily fish such as mackerel and herring are sometimes rolled in oats before being cooked in this way.

Fish steaks and frozen fish products such as fish fingers and fish cakes are also fried.

Heat the butter and oil (you will need about ¼ inch of fat in the pan) until foaming, add the fish and cook over a high heat until the skin of the fish is crisp and the flesh is just beginning to flake. Drain the fish on kitchen paper before serving.

Fillets of fish, thin strips of white fish, dipped in batter, and small fish such as sprats and whitebait are deep fried in cooking oil. Heat the oil until a slight haze rises from it, add the fish (do not overcrowd the fish in the pan) and cook until crisp and golden.

Grilling

Many fish, especially those of the oily variety (herring and mackerel), respond well to being grilled. Large fish should be filleted or cut into 1–1½-inch thick steaks and the smaller the fish or pieces of fish the hotter the grill should be – cooking large fish under too hot a grill will result in the outside being burnt and the inside not being quite cooked enough. Whole fish should be scored through the skin at ¾-inch intervals so that the heat will penetrate through to the backbone.

Brush fish before grilling with melted butter or oil and baste frequently with the juices in the pan during the cooking time.

Steaming

Fish that is to be incorporated with a sauce, left to get cold and then used for a salad or served as a light meal for invalids can be steamed over hot water on a plate set over a pan of hot water. The fish should be covered and is ready as soon as the flesh begins to flake.

Baking

Baking fish in the oven has two advantages; it brings out the natural oils of the fish and avoids the smell of cooking fish in the kitchen. The process is most suitable for oily fish or for white fish that is to be well smothered with liquid or vegetables in order to add extra moisture. Care should be taken not to overcook the fish which should be removed from the oven as soon as the flesh begins to flake or to come away from the bone.

Basic recipe

1. Brush the prepared fish with vegetable oil or melted butter and season it with lemon juice, salt and freshly ground black pepper. Whole round fish should be lightly scored through the skin in a few places. Place the fish in a well-buttered or oiled baking dish and cook in the centre of a moderate oven (350°F/180°C Reg 4) and allow 25–30 minutes for whole fish and about 15 minutes for thick fish steaks. Baste the fish frequently with the juices in the dish during the cooking time. Instead of using butter or oil the fish can be wrapped in fatty rashers of streaky bacon and then lightly brushed with butter before baking.
2. The fish can be wrapped in foil before cooking in the oven which is an excellent way to seal in the aroma and juices of the fish. Place each fish or steak on a piece of well-buttered foil, season with salt and freshly ground black pepper, add a little lemon juice and wrap up in a neat parcel sealing the edges of the foil tightly. Bake in a moderate oven (350°F/180°C Reg 4) for about 20 minutes for steaks and about 8 minutes a pound for whole fish.

Fish cakes

Serves 4
1½ lb cooked, mashed potatoes
½ oz butter
2 tablespoons milk or single cream
6–8 oz cooked white fish, smoked fish or salmon etc.
1 tablespoon finely chopped parsley
salt and pepper
white flour
1 beaten egg
brown breadcrumbs (see page 111)

Remove any skin and bones from the fish and flake the fish with a fork. Melt the butter and beat it into the mashed potatoes with the cream. Season with salt and pepper and mix in the fish and finely chopped parsley.

Using floured hands, shape the mixture into flat cakes about $\frac{1}{3}$-inch deep and 3 inches in diameter. Brush the cakes with beaten egg and coat them in breadcrumbs (spread the crumbs on a flat plate and lightly press each side of the cake into the crumbs).

Fry the cakes in about $\frac{1}{2}$ inch of fat, vegetable oil, lard or dripping for about 3 minutes on each side until they are crisp and golden brown. Turn them carefully to prevent them breaking up. Drain the cakes on kitchen paper.

Variations
Serve the fish cakes with a fresh tomato sauce to make an excellent supper dish.

Add half a teaspoon of mixed dried herbs to the mixture.

Coat the fish cakes in packaged bread stuffing instead of breadcrumbs to make a savoury supper dish.

Flouring whole fish or fish fillets

If fish is to be fried it is often rolled in seasoned flour before being cooked; the effect of flouring the fish results in deliciously crisp and well-flavoured skin.

Mix your seasoning into the flour in a large flat dish – a touch of cayenne pepper to a mildly flavoured fish gives it an extra lift if it is used as well as salt and pepper.

Dry the fish or the fillets well on kitchen paper and press them into the seasoned flour making sure every bit of the fish is well coated.

Egg and breadcrumbing

Fried fish is also often dipped into beaten egg and then coated with breadcrumbs before frying to give a crisp, almost crunchy coating. Use brown breadcrumbs and when possible bake your own crumbs (see page 111) rather than using the impossibly golden crumbs that are commercially produced.

Beat an egg with a little salt. Spread the crumbs over a shallow dish. Brush the fish (using a pastry brush) all over with the beaten egg and then press the fish into the breadcrumbs making sure that every bit of exposed flesh is covered evenly.

How to tell when fish is cooked

It is probably more difficult to tell the exact time that fish should be cooked than to tell the cooking time of any other dish. So much depends on the thickness of the fish but, since it usually requires such a short time, it is usually not too much of a hardship to watch your fish as it cooks and to test it every now and then so that you catch it at just the right time.

To test fish, pierce the thickest part of the fish with a fine skewer. The fish will be tender when the skewer goes easily through to the bone and when the flesh is opaque and easily comes away from the bone. Remember that the fish will go on cooking for a time after you have taken it away from the heat and if you are going to keep it warm for a time before serving it should, if anything, be undercooked when it is removed from the heat.

Garnishings and the final touches for fish dishes

Garnishing really comes into its own where fish dishes are concerned because these tend to be rather on the colourless and perhaps bland looking side. Garnishing takes so little extra time and yet it does do so much to make the fish look more interesting and therefore more appetising. I am convinced that far too many fish dishes of real excellent and high nutritional value are all too often ignored merely because they do not look all that inviting.

Garnish your fish dishes with any of the following:

Lemon wedges and S-shaped slices
Cut a lemon into eight lengthwise slices and remove the pips.

Cut thin slices of lemon and then cut three quarters of the way through in the centre of the slice and twist each cut so that you get an S-shape.

Finely chopped herbs
Finely chop parsley, chives, chervil, spring onion tops or celery leaves to sprinkle over a finished fish dish just before serving.

Watercress and other chopped ingredients
Surround fish dishes, especially if they are cold, with a ring of finely chopped watercress with the stalks removed.

Give colour to fish dishes by sprinkling over some finely chopped red and green pepper with the core and seeds removed.

Sprinkle over the dish some finely chopped dill or fennel leaves or make a pattern with chopped capers, finely chopped pickled walnuts or gherkins or some sieved 'mimosa' egg yolks.

Anchovies
Anchovies make an obvious and surprisingly inexpensive garnish for fish dishes. Divide tinned drained anchovy fillets into two lengthwise and place them in a criss-cross pattern on the dish.

Knowing your fish and when you should be able to buy it

Bass	January–March June–December	Sea fish with a good flavour and white flesh. Grill, bake, shallow-fry or stuff whole.
Bloater	(fresh) September, December (smoked)	Similar to herring. Grill, deep-fry or stuff and bake. Use as smoked mackerel.
Bream	January–March June–December	A stubby silver-coloured fish with a slightly flaky texture and pinkish flesh. Bake whole with stuffing or grill or deep-fry fillets.
Brill	All year round	A flat fish (the poor man's turbot). Poach, bake or grill whole fish or fillets.
Carp	Now quite widely available	Boil, poach or bake whole with stuffing.
Cockles	June–July	Boil and eat fresh or pickle in vinegar.
Cod	January–May, July, August, November, December	Bake, grill steaks, steam, fry etc.

Cod roe	As for cod (smoked) All year round.	Slice and fry. Use for pâtés and dips etc.
Coley/ Saithe	All year round	Fry or grill in steaks and fillets. Use for fish pies and soups etc. Good value – don't be put off by the greyish flesh which whitens on cooking.
Conger eel	March–October	Good taste and usually reasonable in price. Fry in steaks or use in soups and pies.
Crab	January–October (watch out for warm weather when shellfish can be unreliable)	Salads, hot dishes and sandwich fillings.
Crawfish	January–October	Freshwater prawns, boil or shallow fry or grill.
Crayfish	January and February, May–August	Cheaper than lobster but the flesh is just as good providing the crayfish are not too large. Boil or grill.
Dabs	All year round	Very delicious small flat fish with an excellent flavour. Cook smallest fish whole or fillet larger fish.
Eel	All year round	Boil, fry or stew.
Flounder	May–February	Small flat fish similar to plaice. Comes whole or in fillets. Poach, grill, bake or fry.
Grayling	September–December	Bake large fish with stuffing; fry or grill small fish.
Gudgeon	July–November	Grill or fry.

Gurnet	October–July	Bake whole with stuffing or shallow fry fillets.
Haddock	All year round, best from May–February (smoked)	Comes in whole fish, steaks and fillets. Poach, stew, steam, grill or fry. Steam or poach.
Hake	November–August	Whole, steaks or fillets. Bake, fry or grill.
Halibut	All year round	Excellent flat fish with a good flavour but inclined to be a little dry so must have a sauce. Bake whole, grill or fry fillets or poach them.
Herring	April–November	Now becoming scarce and no longer the cheap eating it was. Grill, fry, bake, souse or marinate.
Herring roe	April–November	Fry or poach.
Huss	All year round	Firm pinkish flesh with a light flavour similar to scampi. Deep fry, poach or grill.
Kipper	All year round	Grill, poach or bake. Use for pâtés.
Ling	May–July, September to December	Bake whole, grill steaks, grill or fry fillets.
Lobster	March–October	Boil or halve and grill. Use for salads, in hot dishes etc.
Mackerel (smoked)	December–July All year round	Grill, fry, bake, souse etc. Serve cold or use for pâtés.

Monkfish	All year round, best October–January	A delicious fish despite its ugly appearance. Taste and texture similar to scampi. Grill, bake or fry.
Mullet, Grey	Best July–February	Delicate white flesh with good flavour. Bake whole fish stuffed, grill, fry or poach.
Mullet, Red	Summer	Bright red fish called the woodcock of the sea. Liver should be cooked with the fish. Grill or bake whole or make into a delicious soup.
Mussels	April and May, July–September	Discard any that stay open when shells are tapped before cooking. Boil, fry, grill, use in soups and stews.
Oysters	January–April, September–April	Eat raw; grill, bake, shallow-fry or serve in soups and stews.
Perch	June–January	Freshwater fish with rather a lot of bones. Fry, poach or stew.
Pike	August–March	Freshwater fish that tends to be a little tasteless. Bake whole with a stuffing or use for fish forcemeat.
Pilchards	April–November	Very similar to herrings and can be cooked in all the same ways.
Plaice	All year round	Can be fried or grilled whole or the fillets can be fried, grilled, baked or poached.

Prawns	All year round	Home fished prawns are bright pink – imported prawns or 'shrimps' are much larger. Boil fresh prawns or fry them in a very little very hot oil. Use cooked prawns for cocktails, salads and a number of made up dishes.
Queens	July–April	Use as scallops.
Redfish	June–December	A bright red stubby fish with a bland flavour. Stuff and bake whole or poach, stew or use for soups.
Rock salmon	(see Huss)	
Salmon	March–September	One of the great kings of fish; treat it with respect. Bake or poach whole fish and serve hot or cold. Grill, fry or poach steaks.
(smoked)	All year round	Serve uncooked or in pâtés etc.
Salmon trout	February–August	Poach or bake whole fish.
Sardines – imported		Strong-flavoured small fish. Cook as herrings or barbecue over an open fire.
Scallops	October–April	Fry, poach or use for made up dishes.
Skate	August–April	The wings only are eaten. Fry, steam or poach.
Smelts	October–May	Cook whole. Deep-fry, bake or souse.
Sole, Dover	All year round	Fry or grill whole. Fry, grill, steam, poach or bake fillets.

Sole, Lemon	All year round	Fry or grill whole. Fry, grill, steam, poach or bake fillets.
Sole, Megrim	All year round	Very like a dab in flavour. Serve whole or fillet (the skin tends to be a little coarse). Poach, bake, grill or fry.
Sprats	February and March, October–December	Deep-fry or souse.
Squid and *cuttlefish*	All year round	These need careful cleaning. (Remove the intestine and backbone. Clean inside carefully. Remove the purplish cuttle skin.) The effort is rewarded by the firm texture and subtle flavour. Cut into fine slices and fry.
Tench	All year round or according to river laws.	Another river fish that needs a little extra flavouring to make it into something special. Grill, fry or bake.
Trout	All year round if they are farmed	Grill, shallow-fry, bake or poach.
Turbot	All year round	Another king of fish with a delicious firm but tender flesh. Bake, poach or steam.
Whelks and *Winkles*	April and May	Steam and fry to use in soups or serve with vinegar, salt and pepper.
Whitebait	January–September	Minute little fish that are full of goodness. Flour and deep-fry whole.
Whiting	All year round	Deep fry, grill, poach or bake.

Dairy Foods

Milk

For the last hundred years or so there has been a blanket conception that milk is good for you; now recent research shows that milk actually disagrees with some people and there may be a premise for suggesting that if a child refuses to drink milk it may be because he is one of those who should not drink too much of it. Overall, however, it has long been known that milk does contain a good deal of goodness that we need in our bodies to keep us healthy and fit (protein, vitamins A, B, C and D, small amounts of iron, fat, carbohydrates and calories).

Types of milk

The milk sold in Great Britain has been pasteurised to destroy harmful bacteria. Untreated milk, straight from the farm, is sold in very few places and has a green cap on the bottles. Pasteurised milk which is the mostly widely used has silver tops. Homogenised milk, the easiest to digest and therefore the best milk for the elderly or the very young, has red tops. The richest and creamiest milk is that which comes from the Channel Islands and South Devon cows and is sold in bottles with gold tops – from this milk it is possible to syphon off your own cream.

Sterilised milk, sometimes recommended for small babies, has a slight caramel flavour and will keep, unopened, for seven days; sterilised milk is usually sold in cartons.

'Longlife' milk, also sold in cardboard cartons, has been given an ultra-heat treatment and will keep, unopened, for several months. Powdered milk made from dried milk or a milk substitute is useful to keep in your store cupboard; most brands can usually be used in the powdered form for coffee and reconstituted with water for use as a substitute for fresh milk or for those on low fat diets.

Buttermilk

The liquid left over from making butter or cream. Buttermilk is slightly watery and has a faintly sour flavour but served really cold it makes a good non-fattening drink.

Cooking with milk

When you are using milk for cooking it is best to use the everyday silver-topped pasteurised milk unless you are on a diet when the least fattening of the milk products is powdered milk.

Milk is widely used for cooking. It is essential in the making of most white sauces which include cream, parsley, onion and bread sauces. It is used to add to cream soups of all kinds and is used to make batters, fritters and pancake mixtures.

There are a large number of puddings including bread and butter pudding, Queen of puddings, junket (this must be made with pasteurised milk) and custards which are all based on milk.

Boiling milk

Many recipes call for the milk to be brought to the boil before being added to other ingredients; take care when you do this because milk boils fast and, as it comes to the boil, increases in volume and is inclined to foam over the top of the saucepan – this can be prevented by placing a special glass disc in a milk pan.

Cooking with buttermilk

Buttermilk is lighter than ordinary milk to cook with and can be used to make excellent scones and bread.

Storing milk

Pasteurised, homogenised and other fresh milk should be stored in the refrigerator and should be kept tightly covered as they are inclined to pick up odours from other foods.

Cream

Cream is the fatty part of the milk which rises to the top of the milk when it is left to stand. It is used to make butter and cheese and is also widely used in cooking for both hot and cold, sweet and savoury fishes.
Single cream A minimum of 18 per cent butterfat with a good pouring consistency. Single cream can be used for sauces, thickening soups and for serving with coffee and puddings. It will not whip.
Whipping cream Can be used, whipped, for decorating, pipings and as a filling for sweets. When whipped the cream should double in bulk.
Double cream A thicker, richer cream which does not pour well unless it is absolutely fresh. Double cream is used for making sauces, in puddings and for other recipes and can be increased when whipped by beating in a little milk or by adding some beaten egg white to the whipped cream.
Sour cream Specially treated single cream which is cheaper than ordinary cream and goes well in soups (especially cold soups), sauces and cake-making.
Double cream 'Extended Life' Will keep for 2–3 weeks in a refrigerator but does not really have the essential taste of fresh cream.
Sterilised cream A treated cream with a caramel flavour. It will not whip successfully but can be used for cooking.
Devonshire or Cornish cream Clotted cream is made from milk that has been simmered; the crusty cream is then skimmed off the top. It is used as a filling for scones and is served with fruit puddings.

Cooking with cream
Cream adds a richness to thick soups and sauces. Add it to rich meat, chicken and fish dishes, use it as a garnish to hot and cold soups (swirl a tablespoon of cream into each bowl just before serving). Single cream, seasoned with a little salt and pepper and flavoured with a little lemon juice, makes an excellent dressing for vegetables.

Double or single cream provides a richness and a touch of satin luxury to everyday and special dishes but it must never be allowed to boil. Boiling cream causes it to separate giving either a curdled effect or a liquid butter addition to ingredients. To avoid this the cream should be added to other ingredients just before serving and then heated through (stirring all the time) until it is hot *but not boiling*.

Double or whipping cream adds a touch of the exotic to many puddings and is also used in the making of cold soufflés, mousses and some ice creams. Beat the cream with a rotary whisk or an electric beater until it is stiff and stands in peaks. Be careful not to overwhip double cream as it will quickly turn to butter. Sweetened whipped cream flavoured with a little vanilla essence (*crème Chantilly*) is used as a decoration and as a filling for éclairs, cream buns and sometimes cakes and makes a delicious accompaniment for fresh fruit such as raspberries and strawberries.

Sterilised cream and Cornish or Devonshire cream are not really suitable for cooking.

Sour cream is an excellent flavouring ingredient for many savoury dishes and especially for summer food. If the cream is to be incorporated into a hot dish it should not be allowed to boil and should be added at the last minute just before serving – the cream will add body and richness as well as flavour. Sour cream is not always easy to find and you can use a substitute of single cream into which you beat a small amount of lemon juice.

Yoghurt

Yoghurt is becoming widely used as a replacement for more fattening cream, as a flavouring ingredient and as a breakfast food. Yoghurt is made by combining a culture with milk so that it sours and sets quickly; cow's milk (the most easily available) or goat's or sheep's milk (available from health food stores) can be used. Fruit yoghurts have fresh fruit incorporated in them and can be used as a sweet; most brands are sold either 'sweetened' or 'plain'.

Natural yoghurt refers to a product that is made with a live culture.

Cooking with yoghurt

Yoghurt can be served on its own or with cereal as part of breakfast. Seasoned with salt and pepper and flavoured with a little lemon juice it makes a good salad dressing. Yoghurt ice cream can be made in the same way as ice cream made with a double cream or custard base. It can replace single cream or sour cream in a recipe but care must be taken not to allow the mixture to boil after the yoghurt has been added as it has a tendency to curdle. Mix the yoghurt into a savoury soup, stew or sauce just before serving and heat through without boiling.

Home-made yoghurt
It is easy to make your own yoghurt providing you use homogenised milk and a starter of some 'natural' or 'live' yoghurt.

Recipe to make one pint
1 pint homogenised milk
2 heaped teaspoons 'natural' or 'live' yoghurt

Bring the milk to boiling point. As soon as it begins to rise up the sides of the pan, remove it from the heat and place the pan in a bowl half-filled with cold water.

Spread the yoghurt over the sides of a 1½-pint bowl. When the milk is lukewarm (it should not be either cold or hot to the touch) pour it into the bowl, then pour it back into the pan and into the bowl again. Repeat the pouring process once more, stir well, cover and leave to stand in a warm place (an airing cupboard, the top of a solid fuel stove or a very cool oven (85°–90°F) and leave to stand overnight.

Instead of standing the yoghurt in a warm temperature you can pour it into a slightly warmed Thermos flask to achieve the same results. If you like yoghurt and use it regularly, it would be worth your while investing in a commercial home yoghurt maker which keeps the ingredients at exactly the right temperature.

Butter

There are various types of butter available on the market today and they vary as much in price as they do in quality.

Salted butter Probably the cheapest butter available, much of which is imported. The butter has a fairly strong salt flavour but keeps well and is fine for cooking when you are making savoury dishes.

Slightly salted butter More expensive than salted butter and with a very pleasant flavour.

Farm fresh butter Usually the most expensive butter of all; it has a short life which makes it have a tendency to turn rancid rather quickly. The butter has an attractive golden colour and is served with toast or bread.

Unsalted butter Keeps longer than other butters but is more expensive than salted butter. This should be used in all sweet dishes and it keeps well in the deep freeze.

Butter and margarine combinations By combining butter with margarine you get a mixture which will spread straight from the refrigerator and is ideal for sandwiches.

Softening butter

Sometimes you find you need butter and all there is rests in the refrigerator as hard as a brick. Don't attempt to soften the butter by placing it on the stove – it will melt. Rinse out a bowl with boiling water and dry it well. Put in the butter cut into small pieces and work it with a wooden spoon until it is soft enough to use.

Creaming butter

Cakes and other recipes require butter to be creamed with sugar or other ingredients. Soften the butter if necessary and put it into a fairly large bowl. Cut up the butter into small pieces, add the other ingredients and cream the mixture by beating with a wooden spoon until it is soft, light in texture, pale in colour and the consistency of very thick cream.

This process can be done with an electric hand beater, in a mixing machine or in a food processor.

Butter for pastry-making

The ingredients for pastry-making should be as cold as possible so this is one occasion when the butter can be taken straight from the refrigerator. The firm butter is cut into small pieces and then cut into the flour using two knives until the flour adheres to the butter and the mixture resembles coarse breadcrumbs. This process can also be done in an electric mixer or food processor.

Storing butter

Butter should be kept in the refrigerator but it is inclined to pick up odours of other produce being stored beside it. Whenever possible it should be stored in a separate compartment or should be double-wrapped or sealed in a plastic container.

Remove butter from the refrigerator half an hour before using it for most dishes. Butter for pastry-making, however, should be used straight from the refrigerator.

Butter can be stored for a short length of time in the deep freeze but should be used fairly quickly after removing it from the freezer.

Frying with butter
Butter burns easily so if you are going to use it for frying it is best to combine it with an equal amount of cooking oil; this will provide the taste of butter while preventing it burning too quickly. Once butter has burnt it develops an 'off' flavour and the only thing to do is to throw it away.

Clarified butter
Some dishes call for clarified butter (usually used for sealing over the tops of pastes, potted meat, pâtés and terrines). To clarify butter heat some butter until foaming, remove it from the heat just before it begins to burn and leave to settle for five minutes. Pour the butter through a sieve lined with two layers of muslin – the result should be a clear, yellow liquid with all the white sediment left behind in the cloth.

Herb butters
These make excellent garnishes for grilled or fried meat, poultry or fish dishes and for poached poultry and fish. Herb butters can also be used as sandwich butters in place of butter. The flavouring ingredients are mixed with softened butter and seasonings, the butter is shaped into a roll, wrapped in foil and left to harden in the refrigerator before being unwrapped and cut into thin slices. Herb butters include the following flavourings: garlic, parsley, chive, mixed herb, mustard and lemon.

Adding the final touch to a dish
Extra richness is sometimes added to cream or thick vegetable soups, stews and casseroles by beating in some softened butter in order to give a satin shine to the dish. Add small knobs of softened butter to the other ingredients just before serving and beat hard until the butter has melted and the ingredients are shining.

Cheese

There are so many cheeses on the market these days that it would be impossible to describe them all so I am only going to consider those forms of cheese which are most often used for cooking.
Cheddar A hard cheese of bright yellow gold colour. The flavour varies from mild to strong (New Zealand varieties usually being more on the mild side). Grated, sliced or cubed cheddar cheese is added to a great number of sauces and to other dishes.

Gloucester A hard orange cheese with a good flavour that is useful if you want a dish to taste exceptionally strongly of cheese.
Stilton A strong blue cheese with a soft texture which is incorporated into savoury butters.
Cottage cheese Usually used in salads or cold dishes. The cheese is made from milk and has a grainy texture which can be made smooth by rubbing the cheese through a sieve.
Cream cheese A smooth soft cheese which can be used in the place of cream for thickening sauces and soups and which is incorporated into many recipes including cheese cake.
Processed cheese This is sold, ready sliced, in packets. It cannot be grated but it can be spread over dishes that are to be heated in the oven or grilled.

Serving cheese as a separate course

Cheese and fruit make an excellent alternative to a pudding to round off a meal. Choose varieties which differ in colour and shape (a good delicatessen should let you taste a small sample of cheese that may be strange to you) and arrange them on a platter. An attractive way to display them is to lay them on some vine leaves or large cabbage leaves. Lay a small sharp knife beside the cheese and accompany them with some coarse salt, sticks of celery and some crisp water or cheese biscuits. Butter can be served on the side but if the cheeses are very tasty this should not be necessary.

Some cheese like Camembert and Brie should be served when they are ripe with the inside of the cheese quite runny. Stilton should be well matured and Cheddar-type cheeses should be firm and fairly dry to the touch.

Storing cheese

Most cheese has a short life and it is better to buy it in small rather than large quantities. Store the cheese in a cool larder rather than a refrigerator if possible and cover it loosely with a piece of muslin; if the weather is warm wring out the cloth in cold water to which a few drops of vinegar has been added.

Grated cheese can be frozen or kept in a refrigerator in a screw-topped jar.

Slicing cheese for cooking

It is sometimes difficult to cut cheese into as thin slices as you require but a useful cheese slice is available which will do this to perfection.

Grating cheese
Cheddar type cheeses should be grated through the coarse blades of a grater for salads and cheese to be used as a topping for savoury dishes. Parmesan cheese and other very hard cheeses should be grated through a fine grater. Stale cheese grates more successfully than fresh and grating it can be a useful way of using up ends of cheese which are no longer fit for the table.

Cooking with cheese
If cheese is overcooked in a dish it tends to become tough and indigestible. Cheese should be heated gently and cooked as little as possible after it has melted.

Cheese added to savoury cooked dishes should be finely grated in order to enable it to melt quickly; the amount you use will depend on the strength of the cheese but remember that the flavour will develop during the cooking time.

Cheese should be added to a sauce after the milk and then stirred over a low heat until it has melted.

Grated cheese to be used as a topping for savoury dishes should be coarsely grated (except in the case of Parmesan) and sprinkled in an even layer over the ingredients; extra seasoning can be given by adding a little dry mustard or a pinch of cayenne pepper.

Garnishing with cheese
Many mixed salads benefit from the addition of some coarsely grated cheese.

Cheese sprinkled over a dish which is served in a plain white sauce immediately becomes more attractive. The cheese is then browned under a grill.

Cubed cheese (Cheddar) can be added to vegetable soups.

Grated Parmesan or Cheddar cheese can be added to rich vegetable soups and stirred in until the cheese has melted; grated cheese can also be served separately.

Grated Parmesan cheese provides both a garnishing and flavouring material for many pasta dishes.

Eggs

Eggs are one of the most invaluable foods known to man. A meal in a package, an egg can be served in a hundred and more different ways, its properties enable it to thicken liquids, solidify when cooked, double in quantity when whipped or whisked and to adapt equally well to either sweet or savoury, hot or cold dishes. Eggs are full of goodness and protein (containing vitamins A and B, calcium and iron) and, in their own right, are perfectly delicious.

Contrary to popular belief, eggs can be stored for far longer than a week; they will keep well in a refrigerator for up to three weeks and, for a good many dishes, they should not be used when absolutely fresh. Fresh eggs tend to curdle when boiled, are hard to peel when hard-boiled and their whites will not whisk as well as those of eggs that are over three days old. Eggs stored in a refrigerator should be kept away from the coldest area and should be removed at least half an hour before using.

Egg grades	*EEC egg weight grades*
Large 62g ($2\frac{3}{16}$ oz)	Grade 1 over 70g
	Grade 2 65–70g
Standard 53·2–62g ($1\frac{7}{8}$–$2\frac{1}{16}$ oz)	Grade 3 60–65g
	Grade 4 (Standard) 55–60g
Medium 46·1–53·2g ($1\frac{1}{2}$–$1\frac{5}{8}$ oz)	Grade 5 50–55g
	Grade 6 45–50g
Small 42–46·1 ($1\frac{1}{2}$–$1\frac{7}{8}$ oz)	Grade 7 under 45g

Most recipes using eggs require standard or medium eggs.

There is no truth in the belief that brown eggs are more rich than white eggs – they are exactly the same; the brown eggs just happen to look more attractive.

With present day laws it is unlikely that you will ever buy an egg that is not fresh enough to use. If you have stored eggs yourself for some time you can test them for freshness by placing the egg in a glass of cold water. If it floats it is likely to be bad and should not be used.

Cracking eggs

Tap the side of the egg against a hard surface with a sharp knock, separate the egg shell in half using the thumbs and allow the egg to slide into a basin.

Separating eggs

Many recipes call for the use of just the whites or the yolks of eggs in the method. Crack the shell as above and then pass the yolk from one half of the egg shell to the other allowing the white to strain through into a basin. If separating more than one egg, crack the second one into another basin in case the yolk breaks and mixes with the other white.

Using eggs in cooking

Eggs boiled, poached, fried and scrambled are used in many combination dishes. They also have three other major uses in everyday cooking:

1. The yolks are used as an emulsifying agent in recipes such as mayonnaise.
2. Egg yolks and whole eggs are used in many recipes as a thickening agent and to bind other ingredients. They are also used to coat ingredients which are to be breadcrumbed and fried, acting as a natural glue.
3. Raising and lightening: beaten eggs are used as a rising ingredient for soufflés, batters and cakes. In some cases the eggs are separated and the whites whisked by themselves and in other recipes the whole eggs, beaten, are required.

Boiling eggs

How often have you heard the old cry 'I can't even boil an egg?' In fact it isn't as easy as one would think; like almost every cookery process, boiling eggs successfully needs just a touch of finesse and a modicum of care to achieve perfection. One of the Mitford sisters on being asked to boil an egg *threw* one into a saucepan of boiling water and was surprised when it exploded; eggs are fragile and they have to be treated carefully.

Tastes vary on the amount of time an egg should be boiled and they also need a fraction less cooking time when they are over three days old. Soft-boiled eggs with the white just set and the yolk runny require about 3½ minutes cooking time; an egg that is to be served with the yolk beginning to harden and the white set really firm should be boiled for about 4–4½ minutes.

In these days of kitchen gadgetry it is possible to get automatic egg boilers, but why bother? All you need is a saucepan, some water and heat.

Fill a small saucepan with enough water to cover the eggs you are to boil. Heat the water until it is boiling well and gently lower in the eggs on a spoon. Turn down the heat so that the water is moving but not boiling furiously and cook for 3½–4½ minutes according to taste. Remove the eggs and tap them sharply on the pointed end to prevent them continuing to cook. Boiled eggs should be eaten as soon as possible after they have been cooked and should be accompanied by toast and butter.

Coddled eggs

Some people prefer their boiled eggs to be coddled and for those with a delicate digestion or for invalids this method of cooking the eggs is very successful.

Bring a saucepan of water to the boil. Place the eggs in the water and remove it immediately from the heat. Leave the pan on the side of the stove, but not over direct heat, for 8–10 minutes.

Soft-boiled eggs (oeufs mollets)

Soft-boiled eggs that are half way between the soft egg you have for breakfast and a hard-boiled egg make a very versatile base for a wide variety of first courses, lunch and supper dishes. These eggs can be used in place of poached eggs, they can be used for hot or cold dishes and are more digestible and have a better texture than hard-boiled eggs.

Cold soft-boiled eggs are usually served in an aspic jelly as a first course and in hot dishes the eggs are usually placed on a bed of spinach or some other ingredient and masked with a sauce. The eggs are always served whole and care needs to be taken when peeling them.

Bring a saucepan of water to the boil, add the eggs to the fast boiling water and cook them for 5 minutes from the time the water returns to boiling point. At the end of five minutes remove the eggs, drain off the water and leave them under cold running water for a few minutes until the shells are cool. Tap the eggs gently to break the shell and peel with care.

Hard-boiled eggs

There is an idea that once you put eggs that are to be hard-boiled into boiling water they can stay there for ever without coming to any harm. In fact they need just as much attention as soft-boiled or coddled eggs. If hard-boiled eggs are overcooked they become tough and the white of the egg discolours producing a dark layer around the outside of the egg.

Hard-boiled eggs have numerous uses. They can be useful adjuncts for a picnic, can be pickled, stuffed or incorporated into salad dishes and they make the basis of many other hot and cold dishes. Chopped eggs make a good sandwich filling and both the whites and yolks make an attractive garnish.

Cooking hard-boiled eggs Do not use fresh eggs as these will not peel properly when cooked. Bring a saucepan of water (there should be enough water amply to cover the eggs) to the boil so that it is bubbling vigorously. Gently lower the eggs into the water and turn down the heat to prevent them from breaking. Cook for 10 minutes over a medium heat so that the water is moving but not so activated that the eggs begin to bounce around the pan. Remove the eggs and put them immediately under cold running water until they are cool enough to handle.

If the eggs are not required at once, or if they are to be taken on a picnic in their shells, leave them covered with cold water. Peel the eggs by tapping them firmly against a hard surface and slide off the shells. Peeled eggs that are not to be used for some time should be covered with cold water to prevent the outside hardening.

Using hard-boiled eggs as a garnish All food, and especially summer food, tastes better if it looks attractive. The finely chopped white of hard-boiled eggs and the sieved yolks provide a quick and effective form of garnishing. Eggs can also be sliced or quartered to garnish cold dishes. For slicing you will need an inexpensive egg slicer made from metal or plastic which will cut the egg into neat uniform slices.

Cooking with hard-boiled eggs Hard-boiled eggs can be used to 'stretch' a great many dishes including pies, ingredients served in a white or cheese sauce (e.g. cauliflower cheese) and in their own right for a curry or with a savoury stuffing. The eggs should not be cooked for too long after they have been hard boiled as they are inclined to toughen and dishes incorporating hard-boiled eggs should never be frozen.

Poached eggs

There is an art in making real poached eggs as opposed to using a special poaching pan which really bakes rather than poaches the eggs.

The eggs must be cooked separately; they should be cracked into a cup rather than straight into the pan and the water to which they are added should be boiling vigorously when the eggs are added. Some people add a few drops of vinegar to the water to prevent the eggs breaking up but, in my opinion, this gives them a rather unpleasant flavour and should not be necessary.

Half fill a wide shallow pan or high-sided frying pan with water. Add a pinch of salt and bring to the boil until the water is bubbling vigorously. Create a whirlpool in the water by stirring it with a spoon and slide an egg into the centre of it. Lower the heat a little and cook the egg gently until the white is opaque. Remove the egg carefully with a perforated spoon.

Poached eggs for combination dishes Although eggs cooked by the first method are sometimes slightly ragged around the edges they taste delicious; if the eggs are to be used for hot or cold dishes they can be trimmed with kitchen scissors or, instead of sliding eggs into a whirlpool created in the water, you can set some lightly greased pastry cutters in the pan and slide the eggs into these thereby giving them a neat, circular shape. Eggs that are to be poached in advance should be placed in a dish and covered with cold water as soon as they have been cooked to prevent the eggs from hardening.

Using a poaching pan Eggs poached in special circular cups set in a shallow pan; poached in this way the eggs have a perfect shape but are more like baked eggs than real poached ones. Half fill the pan with water, put a small dab of butter into each cup and heat until the water is bubbling gently and the butter has melted. Slide an egg into each cup, cover and cook until the eggs are just set – 3–5 minutes, depending on the heat of the water. Slide a knife around the eggs to loosen them and turn them out.

Serve poached eggs on hot buttered toast.

Use poached eggs in place of *oeufs mollet* in both hot and cold dishes.

Baked eggs (*Oeufs en cocotte*)

Eggs, broken into individual dishes and baked in the oven, can form the base of a number of quickly prepared and cooked delicious first course, lunch or supper dishes. Care must be taken not to overcook the eggs; they should be cooked for only as long as it takes to set the whites and then served immediately as they will continue to cook for a short time after having been removed from the oven.

4 eggs
butter
4 tablespoons single or double cream
salt and white pepper

Lightly butter four ramekin dishes. Place a teaspoon of cream in the bottom of each dish, break in the eggs, cover with the remaining cream and sprinkle with a little salt and pepper. Place the eggs on a baking sheet and bake in a moderate oven (350°F/180°C Reg 4) for about 8 minutes until the whites are just set.

Scrambled eggs

Scrambled eggs need to be cooked with care if they are to be successful. Don't try to hurry the cooking process or the eggs will curdle and become watery.

Do not overcook the eggs or they will dry out and become tough. Do not stir the eggs too vigorously while they are cooking; they should have a silky, creamy texture.

3 eggs
2 tablespoons single cream, milk or water
salt and white pepper
½ oz butter

Lightly beat the eggs with the cream, milk or water until they are well broken up and smooth but not foaming. Season the eggs with salt and pepper.

Melt the butter over a low heat, add the eggs and cook over a low heat, stirring every now and then with a wooden spoon and turning the edges of the scrambled eggs towards the centre as they begin to set, until all the mixture has thickened. Remove from the heat and continue to stir gently until the eggs have just set and are creamy.

Serve the scrambled eggs on rounds of buttered toast with the crusts removed.

Cold scrambled eggs Cold scrambled eggs make a delicious filling for sandwiches or a topping for Danish open sandwiches. Cook the eggs in the normal way, leave to get cold and then spread to fill the sandwiches. For Danish open sandwiches, cook the eggs in the normal way, transfer them to a small terrine and leave to chill in the refrigerator; turn out and cut into thin slices to use as the topping garnishing with thin rashers of streaky bacon with the rinds removed, cooked without extra fat until crisp and drained on kitchen paper to remove excess fat.

Fried eggs

Fried eggs are the traditional breakfast food of the British. They can also be used to top main course dishes and make a delicious sandwich filling for a packed lunch.

Use a non-stick or smooth-bottomed frying pan; if you are serving bacon with the eggs cook the bacon first so that the eggs can be fried in the fresh bacon fat.

Heat a little lard or oil in a frying pan. When the lard or oil is hot, but not smoking, slide in the eggs, each broken into a cup, and cook without overcrowding over a medium low heat; baste the eggs with some of the fat from the pan so that they cook from the top as well as the bottom, until the eggs are just cooked. Remove the cooked eggs with a fish slice.

Traditionally, fried eggs are served with bacon, fried bread and grilled tomatoes for a hearty breakfast.

Cooked on both sides Some people like their eggs cooked on both sides – it is a matter of taste. Cook the eggs in the fat until they are set firm around the edges. Carefully turn the eggs over, using a fish slice or wide palette knife, and continue to cook until the eggs are just set.

Serving fried eggs as part of a main course Fried eggs can be served on top of hamburgers, steaks, escalopes of veal and some spaghetti dishes. The eggs must be fried at the last minute and the dish served immediately they are cooked.

Fried egg sandwiches Hot or cold fried eggs can be used as a filling for sandwiches or baps. The eggs can be topped by a strip of crisply fried streaky bacon.

Deep-fried eggs

Some recipes call for deep-fried eggs; these are cooked in the same manner as poached eggs with the eggs being slid from a cup into a whirlpool made by stirring some very hot oil. The eggs will consolidate and are cooked over a very high heat until they are crisp on the outside but the yolks are still liquid. Remove the eggs with a perforated spoon.

Oeufs sur la plat

Eggs are fried in butter in individual stainless steel or copper pans until just set and served in their pans.

Using up leftover egg yolks

There are many occasions on which you will find yourself with spare leftover egg yolks. These can be stored in a small container, tightly covered by cling film, and kept in a refrigerator for up to a week. There are numerous uses to which egg yolks can be put and they should never be thrown away. They can be added to cream soups and sauces to add extra richness of flavour and colour. Yolks are used as the basis of a mayonnaise, hollandaise and bearnaise sauce. Home made custards are made with egg yolks as a basis. Mashed potatoes can be enriched by the addition of an egg yolk. An egg yolk beaten up with hot milk and sugar makes a good drink for children and invalids.

Cooking with egg yolks Egg yolks should always be well beaten until smooth before they are used for cooking – this can be done with a fork, a wire whisk or a rotary whisk.

If egg yolks are to be incorporated into a cooked dish the ingredients should not be allowed to boil after the yolks have been added. If they are to be added to a soup or thin sauce a little of the hot liquid should be whisked into the yolks before they are added.

To prevent yolks separating or curdling they should be whisked or beaten into hot ingredients a little at a time.

Omelettes

One of the most sophisticated and yet simple forms of cooking there is. Eggs are beaten, seasoned and cooked plain, or with other ingredients or a filling, to make a light mouthwatering pancake that is served folded in half as soon as it has been cooked. Care should be taken not to overcook the eggs and a perfect omelette should be slightly running in the centre – overcooking will harden and toughen the eggs.

If you plan to eat a lot of omelettes then it is worth-while keeping a pan especially for this purpose. Non-stick pans are ideal and to prevent sticking the pan should not be washed out between cooking but should merely be wiped carefully with a piece of kitchen paper. A 6–7-inch frying pan is ideal for cooking a two egg omelette (usually two eggs are allowed for each serving) and the pan must have a heavy bottom so that the heat spreads evenly.

Do not use too much fat which will make the omelette greasy and do not allow the fat to burn before adding the egg mixture. Heat the pan over a gentle heat before adding the fat and egg mixture. Butter is the best ingredient in which to cook your omelette but you can substitute margarine or bacon fat that is free from blackened specks.

Serves 1

2 eggs
1 tablespoon water
salt and white pepper
¼ oz butter

Beat the eggs with the water using a fork and beating for just long enough to break up the eggs; they should be smooth but not frothy. Season with salt and pepper.

Heat the pan over a low heat for 30 seconds. Add the butter and continue to heat for just long enough to melt the butter. Swirl the butter around the pan and pour in the egg mixture. Cook over a medium low heat, stirring gently with a wooden spatula and drawing the liquid from the sides of the pan to the centre as it begins to set, letting the runny egg flow to the outside. As soon as the eggs have stablised cook the omelette without stirring for 1 minute until it is lightly golden on the bottom and still creamy on the top. Slide the omelette on to a heated serving dish by tipping over the pan, folding it in half as you do so.

Serve the omelette at once.

Omelette fillings Hot fillings for omelettes are usually spread over the omelette as soon as it is cooked and before it is folded.

Egg shells

Surprisingly enough even egg shells have their uses. Crushed shells added to stock with some beaten egg whites will clarify stock, making it amber clear and transforming it from a stock to a consommé which can be served hot or cold and garnished in a number of ways. The stock of course must be a good colour and have a good flavour in the first place; consommé can be made from chicken, duck or beef stock. (See Clarifying stock on page 167.)

Egg whites

Some recipes call for egg yolks only (e.g. mayonnaise or custard) leaving the egg whites available for other uses. Egg whites can be made into meringues or a meringue topping for puddings, they are added to egg shells to clarify stock for consommé and for sorbets or water ices and, beaten, they can be added to whipped cream to make it go further.

Whipping egg whites Take egg whites from the refrigerator an hour before using (they will increase in bulk if they are whipped at room temperature). Beat with a rotary whisk or electric beater until they have about trebled in bulk and are stiff enough to stay in peaks if you lift the whisk from the whites. As an extra test, the bowl in which you whisk the whites may be turned upside down – the whites should not move.

It is possible, however, to overwhip the eggs so that they become dry; as soon as the whites will form stiff peaks, stop whisking. Use whisked egg whites as soon as possible after whisking as they will lose their froth. Egg whites that are to be whisked must be entirely free from foreign matter (e.g. particles of egg yolk). If they are not completely pure they will not whisk successfully.

Folding sugar into egg whites The sugar has to be evenly distributed through the egg whites but must be very lightly folded into the whipped whites or they will lose their bulk. Sprinkle half the sugar over the whites and fold it into the whites using a figure-of-eight movement – a fork is the best implement for this. Add remaining sugar and fold for just long enough to ensure that the sugar is evenly distributed.

Meringue topping for puddings and pies

Put a meringue topping on some stewed fruit and you immediately have an attractive pudding.

2 egg whites
3 oz castor sugar
1¼ lb stewed sweetened apples, plums, gooseberries, rhubarb etc.

Put the stewed fruit into a fireproof serving dish. Whip egg whites until stiff and lightly fold in castor sugar. Top the stewed fruit with the meringue and bake in a medium oven (350°F/180°C Reg 4) until topping is light golden and crisp on the outside.

Bread

There are so many breads on the market that it is often difficult to choose the right kind for the loaf you really need. From the point of view of cooking however white bread is mainly used for making breadcrumbs and sliced white or brown bread is most convenient for sandwiches or for toast.

Here are a few of the different varieties with their uses:
Thick sliced white and brown bread Use for making toast.
Medium sliced white bread Use for making toast and sandwiches.
Thin sliced white bread Use for making sandwiches.
Tin loaf An uncut loaf with a crusty top used for making toast and sandwiches.
Cob loaf A brown loaf with a crushed wheat topping – serve cut into thick slices.
French loaf or Baton Crisp in the oven before serving and cut into thick chunks. A French loaf is also used for making garlic bread.
Cottage loaf A traditional English loaf made with a large circle of dough topped by a smaller circle. The cottage loaf must be used when it is absolutely fresh. Thick slices of the bread are delicious with a farmhouse butter.
Farmhouse loaf An oblong loaf with a crusty topping which is

good for making sandwiches. Do not use fresh bread for sandwiches as it is inclined to crumble.

Granary loaf A brown circular loaf with a nutty flavour; the bread goes well with any meal and is particularly good for making cream cheese or meat sandwiches.

Storing bread

Bread will keep longer if it is stored in a polythene bag in an airtight bread bin; it will keep longer still in a refrigerator and bread also freezes extremely well.

Crusty bread that has gone soft can be crisped up by sprinkling with a little water and then putting it into a hot oven for a few minutes. Frozen bread can be wrapped in foil and defrosted by being put straight into a hot oven for about 30 minutes.

Using up stale bread

Melba toast

This makes a delicious and professional looking alternative to serving ordinary toast or roll with a meal (it is also good news for slimmers providing they don't cover the slender curled slices of toast with lashings of butter).

Use bread from a medium sliced loaf and lightly toast so that the bread is crispening on the outside but has not yet turned colour.. While the toast is still warm, cut off the crusts and slice the bread horizontally through the centre. Bake the thin slices of bread in a moderate oven (350°F/180°C Reg 4) for about 10 minutes until it has curled and is crisp and golden brown.

Making brown breadcrumbs

Breadcrumbs are used as a topping for a great many savoury dishes. They are easy to make and taste infinitely superior to the commercial 'golden' crumbs on the market but they take time; bake your bread therefore when the oven is already being used at a low heat and use stale bread that would otherwise be thrown away.

Place slices of bread, with the crusts removed, in a roasting tin and bake in a slow oven (250°–300°F/120°–150°C) until the bread is crisp through and golden in colour. Cool and crush into fine crumbs with a rolling pin.

Store the crumbs in an airtight jar.

White breadcrumbs
Fresh white breadcrumbs are used in many recipes. They can be made in bulk, using up stale bread, and stored in a freezer. Remove the crusts from a loaf of stale bread and grate the bread through the coarse blade of a grater.

Puddings
There are a number of puddings which use up stale slices of bread; amongst these are: apple charlotte, bread and butter pudding, Queen of puddings and summer pudding.

Making your own bread

Making your own bread is not nearly as difficult as many people think it to be – it does require practice but it is a most rewarding occupation and once mastered the process is really very simple. One thing, however, that is apt to be confusing is the amount of yeast you should use because books sometimes refer to the quantities in measures of fresh and sometimes in measures of dried yeast. Fresh yeast is bought from a baker or a dairy by the ounce. It comes in block form and should be putty coloured, smooth textured and moist. It should smell fresh and slightly fruity and should not be used if it is crumbly, dark or spotted. Dried yeast is bought from grocers or supermarkets in packages or tins and must be kept in an airtight container in a cool dark place once it has been opened. Two level teaspoons dried yeast = ½ oz (15 g) fresh yeast.

Pastry and Batters

Pastry

A great mystique has been created about some aspects of cookery and pastry is in this category, along with making mayonnaise and soufflés. Don't be put off by those cries you often hear of 'I just can't make good pastry'; it is neither difficult nor is it magic – all it needs is a little patience and practice.

Follow these guidelines and, although your first or second shot at pastry-making may not be perfect, you will very soon get the touch.

1. Ingredients for pastry-making, with the exception of the fat, should always be as cold as possible (add a cube or two of ice to the liquid you are going to use to bind your pastry).
2. Make sure your hands, as well as your ingredients, are cool (wash them in cold water before starting).
3. Chill your pastry for a time in a refrigerator before attempting to roll it out and flour the area you are using and your rolling pin well so that the pastry will not stick.
4. Work quickly and handle the pastry as little as possible.
5. Always use plain flour for pastry-making unless a recipe definitely states otherwise.
6. Pastry shrinks when it is subjected to a high heat so be generous when topping pies or lining pie dishes; lift the pastry of

pies from the ingredients by placing a pie funnel or an upside down egg cup in the centre of the dish and leave an air vent in your pie topping to allow excess steam to escape.

What has gone wrong?

If your pastry does not turn out quite to your liking here are some of the reasons why it might have gone a little wrong.

1. Tough pastry: too much liquid and not enough fat was used, the pastry was overhandled, the ingredients were not cold enough or the pastry was overcooked.
2. Crumbling pastry: the pastry was too short, i.e. too much fat and not enough liquid was used or the fats had not been cut properly into the flour.

Rolling out the pastry and lining dishes with pastry

The best surface of all on which to roll out pastry is a marble slab since this stays cooler than any other surface. A slab of marble for this purpose can be bought from a good kitchenware shop but if you haven't got one use a formica surface instead, trying to keep as far away from a hot stove or heater as possible.

Sprinkle your surface and your rolling pin generously with flour. Place your ball of pastry dough on the surface and flatten it with floured hands until it is about $\frac{1}{2}$-inch thick. Always roll pastry away from you turning it around as you roll so that it spreads evenly.

For most recipes your pastry should be rolled to a thickness of about $\frac{1}{4}$ inch.

To line a flan case Dust the surface of the rolled pastry lightly with flour. Fold it in half and place it half-way across your case. Unfold the pastry, press it firmly into the bottom and sides of the case and then trim off the edges with a sharp knife or a pair of kitchen scissors.

To top a pie Choose a pie dish that has flattened edges on the top so that you have something to which the pastry can stick. Fill the pie dish, placing a pie funnel or upside down egg cup in the centre.

Cut a $\frac{1}{4}$-inch wide strip from the rolled pastry. Dampen this with a little water and press it around the top of the pie dish. Brush the strip with a little more water. Cover the pie with the pastry and press it firmly on to the pastry strip with your fingers. Flute the edges with the back of a fork to give an attractive edging.

Most pies are brushed with milk or beaten egg to give a glossy golden effect to the cooked pastry.

The pastry can be decorated with leaves cut out from any remaining pastry. Cut the pastry into leaf shapes and score lightly through the shapes to give the effect of the leaf veins. Damp the leaves with a little water before sticking them to the surface of the pie.

Cut an air vent through the pie funnel or on either side of the centre of the pie.

Definitions of pastry dishes

Pies A pie is a dish in which the ingredients are covered with pastry. The dish may well have pastry both below and above the ingredients.

Flans These are sweet or savoury pastry cases in which the filling is uncovered. Tarts come into the same category.

Quiches Delicious savoury flans in which the ingredients are usually bound with beaten eggs and cream.

Baking blind Some flans that are filled with soft or liquid ingredients are best cooked 'blind'. That is pre-cooked and then filled later; this prevents the pastry becoming soggy and absorbing some of the liquid from the filling.

Line a flan dish or tin with pastry (it should be rolled out as thinly as possible). Prick the bottom lightly with a fork and line the pastry case with greaseproof paper or tinfoil. Fill the case with rusks of bread, dried beans or peas (you can buy special metal beans for this purpose) and bake in a hot oven (400°F/200°C Reg 6) for 10 minutes. Remove the filling and paper or foil and return the shell to the oven for a further 5 minutes until set firm. When it is cold the inside of the shell can be painted with a little beaten egg to give extra protection from the filling.

You can avoid the filling and lining process if you freeze the flan case before putting it in the oven but this does need practice to time correctly and any bubbles in the pastry will need to be pressed out.

The different pastries

Rich shortcrust The most popular of all pastries; it can be used for pies and pastries etc. The addition of an egg yolk makes a richer pastry that has a crisper texture when cooked.

Shortcrust Useful when an easily managed pastry is required for topping pies.
Pâte sucrée A light delicate pastry that is suitable for pies and baking blind. The pastry tends to be a bit difficult to handle and should be left for an hour or two in a cool place before being rolled out. Roll out on a board that is very generously dusted with flour and sprinkle the pastry with more flour as you roll it.
Quiche or flan pastry Suitable for all quiches and savoury flans. Leave to stand in a cool place for an hour before rolling out.
Cheese pastry A little finely grated Parmesan cheese and a pinch of cayenne pepper can be added to shortcrust pastry for savoury dishes.
Puff pastry Rough puff and puff pastry both take a considerable time to make and involve fairly complicated processes. As both these pastries can be bought frozen for a very reasonable price I advise buying them rather than attempting to make them at home.

Rich shortcrust pastry
Suitable for covering pies for sweet or savoury dishes.
8 oz plain flour
6 oz butter
1 egg yolk
2–3 tablespoons ice cold water
pinch salt or 2 teaspoons castor sugar

Sift the flour and salt together in a bowl. Cut the butter into flakes, add it to the flour and rub it into the flour with the thumbs and fingertips until the mixture looks like breadcrumbs. Beat the egg yolk with 1 tablespoon of water, pour it into the centre of the flour and mix it in. Add enough water, a little at a time, to make a stiff dough that forms a firm ball and does not stick to your fingers. If the dough is sticky add a little more sieved flour.

Cover with a floured cloth and leave to stand in a cool place for 20 minutes before rolling out.

Plain shortcrust pastry
Make this the same way as the rich short pastry but leave out the egg yolk and add a little extra iced cold water. This is a slightly easier pastry to make but it has a harder texture than the rich pastry.

Pâte sucrée
This is a tricky pastry to work as it's very short. It takes practice so

don't despair if you don't have a one hundred per cent success the first time. If you are in a hurry use the quiche pastry instead.

8 oz flour
4 oz butter
2 oz castor sugar
2 large egg yolks
1 teaspoon finely grated lemon rind

Sift the flour on to a working surface and make a well in the centre. Very finely chop the butter. Beat the egg yolks in a bowl, add the sugar and butter pieces and beat lightly with a wire whisk to incorporate the ingredients. Pour this mixture into the well and gradually work the flour into the liquid with your fingertips, working as fast as you can.

When all the flour has been incorporated, knead the dough lightly just to make it smooth. Dust the dough with flour, wrap it in a clean cloth and leave it to rest in a refrigerator or very cool place for at least 1 hour before rolling out.

Quiche pastry

A good all round pastry that is easy to work.

8 oz flour
4 oz butter
salt and white pepper
4 tablespoons water

Sift the flour into a bowl and season with a little salt and pepper. Cut the butter into small pieces. Make a well in the flour, add the butter and water and work with the fingertips until the ingredients are smooth and mixed to a firm dough. Dust the dough with flour, wrap in a clean cloth and leave for about 1 hour in a refrigerator or cool place before rolling out.

Note If you have a food processor you will find this an ideal machine for making pastry that does not usually need to be chilled before rolling out.

Basic batters

Basic pouring batter for pancakes, baked batter puddings and Yorkshire pudding:

4 oz plain flour
pinch salt
1 egg
½ pint milk or milk and water mixed

Mix the flour and salt, make a well in the centre and break the egg into it. Mix the egg into the flour gradually beating in the liquid a little at a time. Beat with a rotary whisk until the batter is smooth.

A lighter batter for thin pancakes
Use only 2 oz flour and leave the batter to stand for 30 minutes before using.

A richer pancake batter
Add ½ oz melted butter to the other ingredients.

Fritter batter
Use for fruit or vegetable fritters and for coating fish.
4 oz plain flour
pinch salt
1 tablespoon oil
¼ pint water
2 egg whites

Mix together the flour and salt, make a well in the centre and pour in the oil and half the water. Beat the ingredients until the flour and water are incorporated and then gradually beat in the remaining water with a rotary whisk, continuing to beat until the batter is smooth. Leave to stand for 20–30 minutes, then whisk the egg whites until stiff and fold them lightly into the batter.

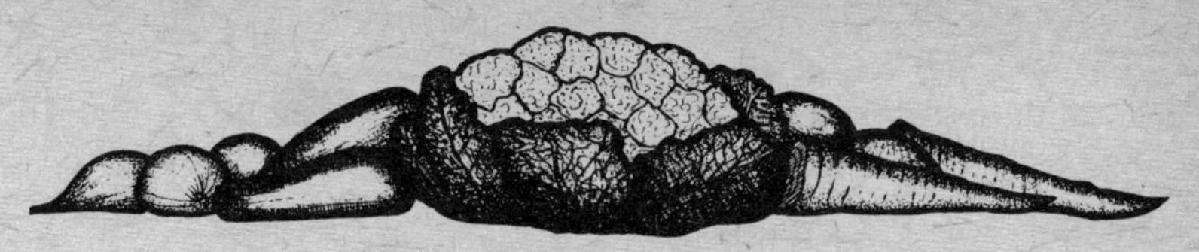

Vegetables

With meat and fish getting more and more expensive, vegetables are really coming into their own and many people are now changing their eating patterns to include very many more vegetable dishes in the place of main course meat, poultry and fish dishes.

The great trick of vegetable cooking is never to overcook them, to cook them as quickly as possible and in as little water as possible without them actually burning. A mixture of vegetables or vegetables served in an interesting sauce can provide good main courses, and vegetables combined with small quantities of meat, poultry and fish can also help to provide substantial dishes for a surprisingly reasonable cost.

If you are buying fresh vegetables ensure that they really are fresh, crisp and not past their prime. Avoid buying them on Mondays and half days when the quality might not be all that good; buy vegetables that have a good colour and a crisp texture and be cautious about buying those that have been prepacked; under these conditions vegetables often tend to sweat, become limp and lose their taste. When buying frozen vegetables make sure that the packs are tightly sealed and that the vegetables inside are free from ice crystals. Frozen vegetables have been blanched so they need far less cooking time than fresh vegetables – the best way of all to treat frozen vegetables is to cook them without water but with a little butter.

Store vegetables in a cool dry and preferably dark place or keep them in the salad compartment of your refrigerator. Remove any bruised or discoloured leaves or stalks before storing. Cook vegetables as soon as possible after you have bought them.

The preparation of vegetables is important. They must always be clean (washed, scraped or peeled as the case may be) and then they must be cooked whole, chopped, sliced, diced or shredded. Try to ensure that your vegetables are evenly cut, that the shredding is uniform, the slices the same size or the matchstick lengths equal in thickness and length. Use a sharp stainless steel knife for preparing your vegetables and cook them as soon as possible after they have been prepared – if the vegetables do have to stand around after preparation, cover them with ice cold water to keep them crisp.

Always *undercook rather than risk overcooking vegetables.* As a general rule, vegetables that grow under the ground are put into cold salted water and brought to the boil and vegetables that grow above the ground are put into fast-boiling salted water.

Root vegetables

Many of the vegetables we eat come into this category which includes most produce that grows below the ground and which provides a high percentage of our winter food. Although roots are sometimes regarded as being rather humble fare they can in fact, if carefully cooked, produce some really delicious and good value dishes.

Much of the goodness of root vegetables lies just below the skin and therefore they should be peeled as thinly as possible. Wash or scrub the roots and peel them with a potato peeler rather than a knife so as to get as thin a peel as possible (left-hand potato peelers as well as right-handed ones can be bought from shops selling kitchen equipment). Some roots are cooked before being peeled and others are baked and served in their skins or, in the case of very young vegetables, boiled and served in their skins.

Leftover cooked vegetables can be used in many re-heated dishes or added to salads.

Most root vegetables are put into cold salted water, brought to the boil and cooked over a high heat until the vegetables are just tender. Some young vegetables are cooked whole but most of the larger roots are sliced, diced or cut into matchstick lengths before or after having been cooked.

Root vegetables respond well to being served in sauces; they can be mashed or puréed, by themselves or combined with other vegetables, with butter and sometimes cream. They need quite lavish seasoning.

Many vegetables, by themselves or combined, form the basis of delicious soups (see soup section on page 172).

Root vegetables are also often added to stews and casseroles. Some can be roasted around a joint or braised with other ingredients. Various roots can be grated and incorporated into salads.

Store root vegetables in a cool dark place and make sure they are dry before storing.

Artichokes (see also Jerusalem Artichokes)

At the end of the last century globe artichokes were grown in every large kitchen garden; then they disappeared from the English greengrocer but now, fortunately, they are brought over by the crate from Brittany and very good they are too. Like asparagus, globe artichokes are 'finger food' but the effort involved is always well rewarded. Artichokes benefit from some careful preparation; there are a great many ways to serve them hot, cold and stuffed and the traditional sauces to serve with the globes are vinaigrette, butter and lemon, hollandaise and a green vinaigrette.

Artichokes discolour as soon as they are cut so use a stainless steel knife when preparing them and have by your side a bowl of cold water with the juice of half a lemon added to it (or rub any cuts with a sliced lemon as soon as you make them).

When you buy globe artichokes they should have a fresh appearance, have few if any discoloured leaves and be firm and springy to the touch. They can be stored for a day or even two by putting the stalks into cold water and leaving them in a cold place.

Globe artichokes have three parts. The outer leaves are dragged through the teeth so that the tender flesh at the base of the leaves is sucked off. In the centre of the artichoke is the 'choke', a circle of hairy fibres which are inedible and have to be removed, and under those are the ultimate prize of the 'fond', a succulent basin of flesh which is the most delicious part of all. The hearts of baby artichokes, picked before the 'choke' has appeared, are tinned in brine. They make good salad material or can be added to casseroles and other made dishes to provide texture and flavour; the 'fond' are also tinned and can be used in the same way. On special occasions tinned 'fonds', which are rather on the expensive side, can be heated in butter and filled with vegetable purée or with cooked peas to make a delicious vegetable dish.

Preparing large globe artichokes for cooking
Break off the tough outer circle of leaves at their base. Using a sharp stainless steel knife, slice off the stalk flush to the bottom of the artichoke. Cut about an inch off the top of the leaves. Plunge the cut artichokes immediately into water to which some lemon juice has been added or rub the cut surfaces with a sliced lemon.

To cook globe artichokes
Prepare the artichokes. Bring a large saucepan of salted water, to which a pinch of bicarbonate of soda has been added, to the boil. When it is boiling really fast, add the artichokes and cook them over a high heat, without covering, for 35–40 minutes. To test, plunge a small pointed knife into the base to see if it is tender. Drain the artichokes and stand them upside down in a colander so that all the water drains off.

To eat artichokes
Pull off the leaves from the outside, dip them in sauce and draw your teeth over the tender, slightly raised part at the base of the leaves sucking off the succulent flesh. Continue to remove the leaves one by one until you get to the smaller leaves in the centre which are not worth bothering about. At this point you will expose the non-edible 'choke'. Using a small sharp knife cut away the hairy fibres and discard them, exposing the soft 'choke' at the bottom. Cut the choke into slices and dip it in the sauce that accompanies the dish.

Artichokes, Jerusalem

These are only a very distant relation to the globe artichoke but they have never been very popular because their knobbly shape makes them difficult to peel. Their flavour, however, providing they are reasonably fresh, is delicious. The artichokes can be steamed, boiled in water or stock or cooked gently in milk. If they are cooked in water they can be cooled and peeled after cooking.

To peel the artichokes, use a small sharp knife and cut the skin as thinly as possible; cut off any small knobbles but try to peel the larger ones. Drop each artichoke tuber as it is peeled into water to which a little lemon juice has been added. The cooked artichokes can be tossed in melted butter, seasoned and mixed with a little finely chopped parsley; they can be sliced and fried in a little butter until they are golden or they can be mashed and mixed with a little butter, cream and seasoning.

Peeled whole artichokes can also be roasted around a joint or a roast chicken in the same way as potatoes.

Asparagus

The rather meagre English supplies of this relation to the bluebell (don't be tempted to try and substitute the bluebell for that is a poisonous plant), which has a very short season, are being supplemented by imports from France, Spain and places even further afield like Mexico and California. The stems of the asparagus vary from thin green and tender stalks to the thicker, often more tough, white variety that need a rather longer cooking time and, if the stalks are very tough, may need to be scraped or peeled before being cooked.

Asparagus freezes well and this often makes a less expensive, though less perfect, alternative to the fresh produce; cheaper still is tinned asparagus which can be used for salads and some made up dishes.

In my mind there is no doubt at all that the best way of all to serve asparagus is as simple as possible – boiled until it is just tender, but not for long enough to make the heads mushy, and to accompany it with a vinaigrette dressing, melted seasoned butter or a hollandaise sauce.

Wash the stalks gently in cold salted water and then carefully skim off the outer coating of the stalk at the point where it becomes fibrous or woody. Cut all the stalks to the same length and tie the asparagus neatly in a bundle. The stalks will cook more quickly than the stems so the best way of cooking is to keep the stems upright in the water with the heads cooking in the steam which rises from the water. If you plan to eat a lot of asparagus then there are special pans for cooking the stems in this way, if not then you can utilise a tall glass jar; place the asparagus in the jar, pour in enough boiling water to come three-quarters of the way up the stems.

Lightly cover the top of the stems with a cap of perforated foil sealed around the jar with string or a large rubber band and stand the jar in a saucepan half-filled with boiling water. Cook for 20–30 minutes, drain off the water from the jar, slide out the asparagus and remove the strings. If you are cooking asparagus in a special pan, half-fill the pan with boiling water, stand the asparagus in the water, cover tightly and cook for about 10–15 minutes until the stalks are just tender. Lift the bundle of asparagus gently from the water and serve as soon as possible.

For a substantial first course allow 6–8 oz asparagus per person.

Eating asparagus

Asparagus is one of those lovely foods for which there is no alternative but to eat with your fingers. Raise your plate by propping it in the front with a fork or spoon placed under it, pour the sauce on to the side of the plate and pick each asparagus stem up by the end, biting off the head and then sucking all the tenderness out of the stem.

Asparagus vinaigrette

Cook the asparagus as above, leave it to get cold and then serve it with a vinaigrette dressing (see page 144).

Asparagus as a garnish

Asparagus tips are often used as a garnish for both hot and cold dishes. For this purpose asparagus tips can be bought in tins or you can cook fresh asparagus; cut off the tips to use as a garnish and use the stems for soup or in a soufflé.

Beans, broad

Of all the bean family the broad bean is probably the most versatile as it can be used in all its stages and its mild, nutty flavour responds well to any number of treatments. Traditionally broad beans are cooked with savory and if you, like myself, like the flavour of this herb it is well worth keeping a small pot of savory on your windowsill. Dried savory can be used in the place of the fresh herb but it will benefit from being soaked in a little lemon juice before being added to the beans.

Ways to use broad beans

1. If you grow your own beans and nip out the tops of the plants in order to make the rest of the plant bush out, don't throw the

top six inches away. The tender young leaves and the young flowers can be plunged into boiling water and cooked like spinach to make the most delicious vegetable. Dress the cooked bean tops with melted butter, a touch of lemon juice, salt and freshly ground black pepper.

2. Very young broad beans, no longer than 5 inches, can be cooked whole in the same way as French beans.

3. Young broad beans are podded and cooked in their skins.

4. Fully matured beans are podded and cooked in their skins but, if the skins are tough, they will have to be removed before serving.

Young broad beans are delicious raw, and both young and skinned mature beans are delicious cold in salads. Broad beans also make a delicious soup.

Allow 8–12 oz unpodded broad beans per serving and 4 oz podded broad beans per serving.

Cook broad beans in boiling salted water for 5–20 minutes until they are just tender.

Beans, French

I happen to prefer French beans to the more prolific runner beans. They have to be eaten when they are young and tender or they might as well be ignored because their flavour deteriorates and they require a long cooking time and stringing rather than just topping and tailing. French beans in their prime require only a short cooking time, their flavour is delicate and almost nutty and they make the most ideal vegetable accompaniment to almost any summer dish. Cooked and cooled French beans, dressed in a vinaigrette dressing, make a delicious salad and the cooked beans are also an essential ingredient of that marvellous dish Salade Niçoise (*see* below).

To cook French beans

Choose young bright green beans that are crisp and will snap easily in half. If the beans are flabby don't buy them. Allow 4–6 oz beans per serving. Top and tail the beans by cutting off about $\frac{1}{8}$ inch from each end. Cook the beans in boiling salted water over a high heat for 5–8 minutes until they are just tender but still retain a certain crispness. Drain the beans well, refresh them under cold running water to halt the cooking process and re-heat them in melted butter. Season with salt and freshly ground black pepper.

Beetroot

Many people seem to consider that the beetroot is a salad or pickle vegetable and you most often meet it boiled and sliced or diced in a salad or preserved in vinegar to serve with cold meats. In fact the sweet, earthy flavour of the beetroot makes it an excellent hot vegetable as well. Many greengrocers sell beetroot ready cooked and peeled which is a relief as the juices stain your hands when you deal with them and they need long cooking.

To cook beetroot wash the roots gently in cold water without peeling them or piercing the skin. Cover the roots with cold water, bring to the boil and cook for one to four hours depending on the size of the root. Test for tenderness by pressing the root gently and if the skin splits and is easy to peel off the beetroot should be tender. Beetroot can also be baked in the oven (wrap the roots loosely in buttered foil and bake them from 1–4 hours until they are tender). Leave cooked beetroot until cool enough to handle and then slide off the skins. Use rubber gloves if possible when preparing beetroot.

Cooked young beetroot can be tossed whole in butter and finely chopped parsley seasoned with salt and freshly ground black pepper. The older roots can be sliced or diced and cooked in the same way but, because of their high sugar content, the best way to serve beetroot hot is to incorporate it into a fairly sharp or well-flavoured sauce.

Brassicas, the

This is the cabbage and cauliflower family of which one or other variety is usually on sale throught the year. Cabbage has always had a bad reputation in the culinary world but in fact it is one of the most useful and least expensive vegetables on the market today. Providing cabbages are not overcooked, there is none of the unpleasant smell associated with cheap boarding houses and bad-tempered landladies, and the flavour of the vegetable can be very good indeed.

Winter cabbage

The great standby of the winter months with its firm heart and dark green outer leaves. Available from October to February. The cabbage leaves can be shredded with the hard core removed and cooked in a little salted boiling water until just tender, well drained, returned to a saucepan with a knob of butter, seasoned with plenty of black pepper and tossed over a low heat until the butter has melted and been absorbed into the leaves.

Colcannon

A delicious way of using up leftover potatoes and cabbage.

leftover cooked cabbage
leftover mashed potatoes
salt and freshly ground pepper
1 oz butter
1 oz lard (or 2 tablespoons bacon dripping)

Shred the cabbage and mix it with the potatoes. Season well with salt and freshly ground black pepper. Heat the butter and lard or the bacon fat in a frying pan until melted and very hot. Add the potatoes and cabbage, press them firmly into the pan with a spatula and cook over a high heat until the bottom of the flat cake is golden brown. Cover the pan with a lid and cook over a medium heat for 20 minutes. Invert the cake on to a heated serving dish and serve with sausages, bacon, roast pork etc.

Savoy cabbage

A paler coloured variety of cabbage than the winter variety, with crisp crinkly leaves, which is available from November to February. Cook in the same way as winter cabbage or use in the place of lettuce during the winter. The leaves can also be steamed and stuffed or the whole cabbage steamed, the centre taken out and a cooked meat mixture packed into the middle before the whole thing is braised in the oven.

Drumhead cabbage

An extremely firm white cabbage which is imported during the winter months and sold by the pound. Ideal for winter salads, especially for making coleslaw.

Red cabbage

This firm dark red cabbage, available from November to March, is usually pickled to serve with cold meats; the cabbage is finely shredded with the core removed, sprinkled with salt and left to stand for 24 hours, drained and then covered with a vinegar and spice marinade.

Red cabbage does, however, also make an excellent winter vegetable if it is cooked in a little stock (after having been shredded) over a low heat with some finely chopped fat bacon, some chopped cooking apple and a few caraway seeds. Red cabbage cooked in this way is a traditional accompaniment for pork, goose and game dishes.

Curly kale, greens and turnip tops
Although these all make perfectly acceptable green vegetables they do tend to have a somewhat strong flavour. Cut out any coarse stems and be careful not to overcook the leaves. Dress them with butter, seasoning and a little lemon juice.

Brussels sprouts
The traditional accompaniment to roast turkey on Christmas Day and one of the most delicious of winter vegetables if properly cooked. Brussels sprouts can also be puréed, used in colcannon or bubble and squeak in the place of cooked cabbage and shredded to serve in winter salads. When the sprouts are small tight spheres they have the delicacy of miniature cabbages but if they are allowed to get large and blousey their flavour deteriorates rapidly.

To prepare Brussels sprouts trim off the coarse base of the stalk, remove any damaged or coarse outer leaves and wash the sprouts in salted water. (Some people like to score a cross through the bottom of the sprouts to speed up the cooking process but I would not recommend doing this unless the sprouts are old and tough.) Bring a pan of lightly salted water to the boil, add the sprouts and boil them for 8–12 minutes until they are just tender but still crisp.

Drain them really well in a large sieve or colander and then toss them in melted butter with a little more salt and plenty of freshly ground black pepper.

Sprouts as a salad ingredient The crispness and light flavour of sprouts make them an excellent winter salad ingredient when lettuces are scarce or very expensive. Wash and trim the sprouts as for cooking and then shred them finely. Mix the sprouts with a vinaigrette dressing or use them in the place of cabbage for a coleslaw salad.

Cauliflower
The white florettes of the cauliflower are tender and respond best to being steamed but don't make the mistake of cutting off all the green leaves that surround the florettes as these also have an extremely good flavour and food value. Leave on the inner tender leaves that fit snugly around the head.

Wash the cauliflower well, remove the coarse outer leaves, cut off any blemished or bruised florettes and soak the head for 10 minutes in very cold salted water to make sure any slugs or bugs are encouraged to leave the florettes. Drain well and cut a cross through the stalk to ensure even cooking. Put one inch water in a saucepan large enough to hold the cauliflower, add a little salt and bring the water to a fast boil. Add the cauliflower, stem end down, return to the boil, cover tightly and cook for 10–15 minutes until the florettes are just tender – do not overcook as this will ruin both the flavour and the goodness of the dish. Drain well, season with salt and pepper and pour over a little melted butter.

For dishes that only require the florettes of the cauliflower, trim off the leaves and the bottom of the stalk and divide the head into florettes. Steam the florettes over boiling water for about 5–7 minutes until they are just tender but still crisp.

Cauliflower can be combined with other vegetables in both hot and cold dishes. It can be mixed into a cheese sauce to make a cauliflower cheese, served hot with a hollandaise sauce or incorporated into a great many salads. Uncooked cauliflower florettes can be served with dips as an accompaniment to cocktails or as part of an assortment of raw vegetables to be served with garlic mayonnaise as a summer starter.

Broccoli/calabrese

Cauliflowers are called broccoli in the West Country but elsewhere the term usually refers to the green and purple broccoli spears or sprouting broccoli, the slightly paler calabrese and the smaller cauliflower. Like cauliflower, these spears are tender and should not be overcooked; cooked to a degree however when they are tender but still crisp, they can be absolutely delicious as a vegetable, incorporated into a main dish or served cold with a vinaigrette dressing or mayonnaise.

Trim off the tough bottom stalks of the broccoli and divide them into florettes. Wash them well and either steam them for about 8 minutes until just tender or cook them in a little boiling salted water for about the same time. Drain the spears well. Older spears should have their stalks peeled and, to prevent the delicate flowers of the young sprouting broccoli breaking up, you can tie the stalks into bundles before cooking.

Carrots

Young and old carrots have quite a different flavour and a different role to play in the kitchen. The young carrots, no more than about six inches long, have a sweet fresh flavour and need only to be scraped or scrubbed, lightly boiled and then tossed in a little butter, seasoning and parsley to make a delicious vegetable – it is a shame to serve them in any other way. The old mature carrots, on the other hand, respond well to any number of recipes; they have a good taste and are invaluable as a vegetable addition to stews and casseroles providing extra flavour. Use the peelings from old carrots to give body to stocks.

Carrots also make an excellent soup and crisp roots, cut into matchstick strips, can be served as part of a warm weather *hors d'oeuvres* (*crudités*) with a garlic mayonnaise or with a savoury dip as an accompaniment to drinks. Grated raw carrot is added to a variety of salads. For some dishes large old carrots may have to have the hard inner core removed. Slices of carrots can be cut to resemble flowers and cooked to use as a garnish. Miniature diced carrots are often incorporated into the base of sauces.

Peel carrots with a potato peeler to remove as thin a layer of peel as possible.

Note Old carrots tend to absorb a lot of water while cooking so take care they are not burning. Always check carrots while they are cooking.

Celeriac

An ugly looking root vegetable that has the flavour of celery and a good firm texture. Once it is peeled celeriac quickly goes brown so it should be covered immediately with a mixture of cold water and lemon juice. The vegetable can be chopped, cooked until tender and puréed or it can be cut into strips, cooked until tender and tossed in butter and lemon with seasonings, served in a white or cheese sauce or left to get cold and served in mayonnaise as a salad ingredient.

Celery

Celery, like so many other vegetables, has made great advances from a cultivation point of view over the years. Now you can buy it almost all the year round and the self-blanching varieties make life much easier for the amateur gardener. When buying celery choose bunches that are pale in colour, thick and hearty, not discoloured and obviously crisp.

The flavour of celery is strong and very individual and any leaves or trimmings make an excellent flavouring ingredient for stock.

Crisp stalks of raw celery are traditionally served with cheese or they can be sliced and added to salads or cut into two inch lengths and stuffed with cheese mixtures. Chopped celery is added to stews and casseroles and the stalks or whole heads are braised to serve as a vegetable.

To prepare celery for cooking trim off the base and the top of the stalks with the leaves attached. Wash the celery in plenty of cold water or divide the stalks, trim off any strings from their sides and scrub if necessary.

Celery as a garnish

Chopped celery leaves can be used as a garnish for any cold dishes, for soups and also to stir into stews at the last minute in the place of chopped parsley. Sprays of leaves can also be deep-fried until crisp and drained on kitchen paper to garnish meat, poultry and fish dishes.

Attractive celery curls can be used to garnish cold dishes. Cut trimmed celery stalks into two-inch lengths. Split the top of the lengths, three-quarters of the way down the stalks, at $\frac{1}{8}$-inch intervals and drop the lengths into a bowl of iced water leaving them until the tops curl outwards giving a flower effect.

Chicory

This slightly bitter plant is blanched to keep the leaves white. It usually makes its appearance as a salad vegetable but the chicory heads can also be braised when they make a well-flavoured vegetable dish.

Corn on the cob, sweet corn or maize

Another vegetable which is fast gaining popularity. Corn on the cob should be cooked when it is as fresh as possible. When buying the corn look for bright yellow, plump kernels and fresh green leaves.

To prepare the corn for cooking
Cut off the stalk of the corn and pull some of the tough outer leaves off. Place the corn in a saucepan, cover with boiling water, add ½ teaspoon salt, return the water to the boil and cook over a high heat for about 5 minutes until the kernels are tender and can easily be pulled off the husk. Drain, strip off the outer leaves and the silky fibres inside and serve the corn with plenty of melted butter.

To eat the corn off the cob
It is possible to buy small pointed handles to insert into each end of the corn on the cob. Otherwise use forks or fingers. The corn is drenched in melted butter and the kernels chewed off the cob. Seasoning is added as required.

Recipes that require the kernels off the cob
For these recipes the kernels can be stripped off the cooled cooked cobs with a small sharp knife but since this is rather a performance I would suggest buying the kernels, ready cooked, in tins. Sweet corn is sold as creamed corn or as just plain kernels and these are the ones you will usually require.

Courgettes and marrows

Over the years the rather insipid and watery marrow has been replaced by the crisper and smaller courgette which is treated in exactly the same way as the marrow but which does not contain so much water and which has a far better flavour. These vegetables are also called zucchini and come in both green and golden varieties.

Ideally courgettes should not be more than eight inches long. They should be crisp, feel firm to the touch and be a bright green in colour (except in the case of yellow or golden courgettes). Courgettes need very little cooking. They can be sliced and fried, combined with another vegetable and stewed or cooked in a fritter batter; they can be thinly sliced and incorporated into a mixed salad or stuffed with a savoury or vegetable filling and served as a first course, main course or vegetable accompaniment. Like aubergine and cucumber, courgette slices can be sprinkled with salt and left for 30 minutes to draw out the water before being dried and cooked.

Small marrows can be treated in the same way as courgettes but large marrows need to be skinned with the seeds removed and the flesh, salted and drained, and then gently stewed in butter to produce an acceptable but not very well-flavoured vegetable.

Courgettes are not usually peeled before being cooked as much of their flavour lies in the skin. They should be washed and dried before being prepared.

Cucumbers as a cooked vegetable

Cucumbers haven't really been used as a salad vegetable for all that long. Up until the end of the last century their role was far more that of a vegetable, with the peeled cucumber being cut into fairly thick sticks or cubes, stewed gently in butter and flavoured with salt, pepper and parsley or chopped chives.

Cucumber can also be cooked in the same way as courgettes (see page 132).

Kohlrabi

These curious looking sputnik shaped bulbous vegetables are not often seen in the greengrocers but they are easy to grow in a vegetable garden and make delicious eating. The leaves of the kohl rabi can be cooked like spinach and the swollen stalks should be picked when they are not larger than the size of golf balls. Cut off the leaves from the bulbous stalks and cook the kohl rabi in boiling salted water for about 20 minutes until just tender. Peel off the skins when the kohl rabi are cool enough to handle, slice the flesh or cut it into matchstick lengths, toss them in butter and sprinkle with parsley, a little lemon and a seasoning of salt and freshly ground black pepper.

The flesh of the kohlrabi can also be coarsely grated and used as a salad ingredient.

Mushrooms

Mushrooms are another vegetable that have so many and varied uses that it is difficult to know where to start with them, what to put in and what to leave out.

As food value mushrooms have probably less to offer than almost any other vegetable, but they do have a pleasant, often slightly meaty, taste. Mushrooms go well with almost any other ingredients; they can be fried, grilled or sliced and served raw in salads. The peelings of extra large mushrooms can add flavour to stocks; chopped mushrooms are indispensable to many sauces and they can be served as first courses, as a vegetable and as a savoury.

Commercial mushrooms come in two basic sizes, small and large, and they are exactly the same species as those found in country fields during the end of summer. The small button mushrooms retain their colour and have a mild flavour and a firm texture. The larger open mushrooms display their pink-beige gills below the cap which eventually becomes black when the mushrooms are very large indeed. The larger mushrooms tend to release their juice during cooking which can discolour other ingredients but if the mushrooms are cooked over a high heat this liquid will usually evaporate.

The dried mushrooms you find on sale in many delicatessen shops are usually dried sep (toadstools as opposed to mushrooms) and have an extremely strong meaty flavour when they are soaked for some time. They are very useful to keep in the larder and only a few will give a great lift to a stew or casserole.

Some recipes require the use of the caps only; the stalks can be used for soups or for adding flavour to stocks.

Mushrooms should never be washed. Their caps may need wiping with a damp cloth but actual washing will impair their flavour. Cook mushrooms for as short a time as possible to retain their texture as much as possible (unless of course they are being incorporated into a mixed dish) and add a little lemon juice to preserve their colour.

When you buy mushrooms make sure they are firm, fresh-looking, crisp and free from too much dirt. Avoid those that are flabby, shrivelled or wrinkled.

Do not season the mushrooms with salt until they are cooked as salt tends to draw out their juices.

Onions

The onion family is another large one which includes varying sizes of these strongly flavoured vegetables from the mini spring onion to the giant Spanish onion. Onions are essential in cookery; not only do they compliment the flavour of other ingredients but they make many good recipes in their own right. Onion skins help to add flavour and colour to stock, chopped chives or spring onions add colour and flavour to cold dishes and a little grated raw onion can make all the difference to a rather bland dish.

It is better to use small rather than large onions (unless they are the Spanish variety) and avoid any that have any sign of green leaves sprouting from the top. Onions must be very firm and should be stored in a cool dry place.

Chives Thin stalks with a delicate onion flavour which are used mainly in salads. Remove any flower heads or yellowed stalks and chop the chives with kitchen scissors.

Spring onions (sometimes called scallions or chipples) These are also mainly used in salads when they are either served whole or chopped. The green part of the onion can be chopped and used in the place of chives and the onions can be cut into lengthwise strips and incorporated into some cooked dishes. Spring onions are not often used after the bulb has grown to more than the size of a large pea. Cut off the bottom and roots of the spring onions and the top inch or two of the stalk. Remove the outside layer of the onions. Store in the salad compartment of the refrigerator.

Pickling onions Small white and yellow onions which are used for pickling, garnishing and in some dishes. Peel the onions before using.

Shallots Usually about the size of a walnut, shallots can be white or slightly purple. They have a strong flavour and are used in many sauces and some other dishes in the place of onions. Cut off the top and bottom of the shallots and remove the peel. When used for sauces the shallots should be very small indeed.

Spanish onions These are the giants of the family and have a milder flavour than normal onions. They can be baked in their skins and are good, cut into rings, for salads.

Peeling and preparing onions

Cut off the top and bottom of the onions and remove the skins with a knife. (Use the skins for stock; when onions are added to stocks wash but don't peel them.) If you have trouble with tears when doing onions, they can be peeled under running water.

Slice onions across the grain from top to bottom. For onion rings, cut the onions into slightly thick slices and then divide into rings.

To chop onions Cut the peeled onion in half and lay it flat side down on a chopping board. Cut the onion into thin slices keeping the shape together and then cut into equally thin slices from top to bottom ending up with the onion finely chopped.
To cook chopped onions Many dishes call for chopped onions to be cooked before other ingredients are added. Cook the chopped onions in a little fat or oil, over a low heat, stirring every now and then to prevent sticking, until they are soft and transparent.

Fried onions
Fried onions are used as an accompaniment to many dishes. They can also be coated in flour in order to give a crisp texture or the rings may be dipped in batter to give a fritter effect.

Cut the onions into thin slices and divide into rings. Heat about $\frac{1}{4}$ inch vegetable oil or dripping in a heavy frying pan, add the onion separated rings and cook over a medium heat, moving every now and then, until the onions are soft and a pleasant nutty brown. To crisp the onions, cook them over a high heat until brown and crisp, drain them on kitchen paper, spread them on a baking sheet and dry them off in a moderately hot oven (375°F/190°C Reg 5).
Crisply fried onion rings Cut Spanish onions into thin slices and separate into rings. Dip the rings in milk and then into flour seasoned with a little salt and pepper. Drop the rings, a few at a time, into deep hot fat or oil and cook them until they are golden brown and crisp. Drain the rings on kitchen paper.

Parsnips

During the winter months parsnips can provide an inexpensive alternative to potatoes. The best parsnips are the younger ones that are not more than eight inches long, but even the larger roots are full of flavour and can be used to make a great many very tasty vegetable dishes.

To prepare parsnips for cooking, trim off the top and bottom of the roots and peel off the skin as thinly as possible. Cut the roots into slices, chunks or matchstick strips depending on how you plan to cook them.

Parsnips can be sliced, steamed until tender and served in a white sauce. They can be sliced, steamed and cooked in a fritter batter; chopped, boiled until tender, drained and mashed with butter, a little cream and seasoning (they can also be combined with mashed potatoes or swede) or they can be cut into chunks, par-boiled for five minutes, drained and roasted beside a joint.

Peas

Providing they are picked while still young, tender and moist, before they have been allowed to dry out and harden, peas must surely be one of the best summer vegetables ever. Peas also freeze and reheat well. You can also buy peas dried and in tins but, for my choice, the young peas from the garden are by far the most superior.

Allow 8 oz peas in the pod for each serving and 3–4 oz frozen peas per serving.

Preparing and cooking peas
Shell the peas by running your thumbnail down the side of the pod, splitting it open and then scraping the peas into a bowl. Home-grown peas can be very uneven in size and it is worth dividing them into small and large to avoid uneven cooking. Like all vegetables peas should not be overcooked and in fact need a few minutes only, if they are young, to tenderise them.

Boiling peas
Shell the peas and cook them in boiling salted water for 8–10 minutes. Drain the peas as soon as they are tender. The peas can be cooked with a sprig of mint in the water and seasoned with salt and pepper before being served. Alternatively the mint can be chopped and added to the drained peas with some melted butter. Cream and a seasoning of salt, pepper and a little ground mace or ground nutmeg can be added to the cooked peas.

Mange tout or sugar peas
Another vegetable that is becoming more popular is mange tout or sugar peas (slim pods with mini peas inside that are cooked whole rather than being podded and must be eaten when they are very young and tender). Mange tout peas are now being grown in England and will, I hope, become readily available.

To prepare the peas, top and tail them and strip off any strings from the sides of the pods. The peas should be cooked in boiling salted water for about 5 minutes until tender but still crisp, drained and tossed in a little seasoned butter.

Potatoes

There has been so much written about the potato and so many dishes devised to utilise it that it is difficult to know quite where to start and where to finish. As a compromise I have included the basic methods of cooking potatoes and some of my favourite recipes.

During recent years potatoes have ceased to play quite as large a part as they used to in the British diet. No longer the cheap commodity they were, potatoes to quite a large extent, have been replaced by less expensive pasta and by other vegetables. Nevertheless, despite changing eating habits, potatoes still remain one of our most popular and versatile vegetables; the new tubers are greeted with pleasure each year and the old potatoes carry on right through the winter.

As with other vegetables, much of the goodness of the potato lies just below the skin and so they should be peeled, with a special peeler, as thinly as possible. Old potatoes may have to have the blemishes and 'eyes' cut out and potatoes for boiling can be roughly chopped for quicker cooking. The water in which potatoes are boiled can be used as a base for soup. As well as boiling, potatoes can be chipped and deep-fried, baked in their skins, mashed and puréed, sliced and fried, or layered and baked in the oven. They can be roasted around a joint, cooked and fried, or peeled, chopped and added to casseroles and stews. New potatoes can be scraped and boiled or just washed and scrubbed and cooked in their skins.

Basic methods of cooking potatoes

Boiling potatoes Choose potatoes of roughly equal size and do not boil potatoes that are very large unless they are to be mashed later – large potatoes can be roughly chopped into even-sized pieces after peeling.

Peel the potatoes and drop them straight into salted water. Drain the potatoes, put them in a saucepan, add ½ tablespoon salt to each quart of water, bring them to the boil, cover and cook them for about 30 minutes or until the potatoes, tested with a fork or narrow knife, are entirely tender. Drain the potatoes well, place them in a serving dish, dot them with a little butter and if desired sprinkle them with a little chopped parsley.

To mash potatoes Place the cooked potatoes in a clean saucepan. Add a knob of butter and a tablespoon or two of milk or cream, season with salt and pepper and mash over a low heat, using a potato masher, until the potatoes are smooth and creamy. Alternatively they can be put through a food mill and then returned to a clean pan with the butter, milk or cream and seasoning.

Pommes mousseline

This is merely a richer version of ordinary mashed potatoes with a flavouring. The potatoes are also of a thinner consistency than the normal mashed potatoes.

Serves 4

1½ lb mashed potatoes
1 oz butter
½ pint milk
grated rind of ½ orange
salt and white pepper
pinch of ground nutmeg

Combine the milk and orange peel and bring to the boil. Put the mashed potatoes (having been finely mashed through a food mill rather than been pounded with a potato masher) in a saucepan with the melted butter. Beat well with a wooden spoon and gradually blend in the boiling milk, a little at a time, beating all the while. Season with salt, pepper and a touch of grated nutmeg and pile on to a serving dish.

Duchesse potatoes

An egg is added to mashed potatoes and the rather stiff mixture is then pipped on to a baking sheet and baked in an oven until the rosettes are crisp and golden brown.

Serves 4

1 lb potatoes, mashed
2 oz melted butter
1 egg
salt and white pepper
touch of grated nutmeg

Add the butter to the hot mashed potatoes (they should be mashed until very smooth) and beat with a wooden spoon. Beat the egg until smooth and gradually beat it into the mashed potatoes. Season with salt, pepper and nutmeg and pipe the mixture through a forcing bag with a large rosette nozzle on to a lightly greased baking sheet. Pipe into rosettes about 1½–2 inches in diameter and about ¾–1 inch high and bake in a hot oven (400°F/200°C Reg 6) until golden brown and crisp – about 20 minutes.

Potato croquettes
Serves 4
1 lb mashed potatoes
1 oz melted butter
1 teaspoon finely chopped parsley
salt and white pepper
1 standard egg
1 small egg
browned breadcrumbs
fat or oil for deep- or shallow-frying

Add the melted butter to the potatoes and mix well. Beat the large egg until smooth and beat it into the potatoes with the parsley. Season with salt and pepper and chill the mixture. Roll the mixture into neat sausage shapes about 1 inch in diameter and 2 inches long, coat them in the small egg, beaten until smooth with a little salt, and then roll them in breadcrumbs.

Fry the croquettes in deep or shallow fat until crisp and golden brown on all sides and drain them on crumpled kitchen paper.

To fry cooked mashed potatoes Heat 2 tablespoons bacon fat or dripping in a large heavy frying pan, add the potatoes and press them firmly into the pan and cook over a high heat until the potatoes are crisp and golden brown on the bottom. Cover the pan with a serving plate and inverse the potatoes on to the plate.

To fry cooked boiled potatoes Cut the cooked and cooled potatoes into ¼-inch thick slices. Melt 2 tablespoons dripping, bacon fat or vegetable oil in a frying pan and cook the potatoes over a high heat until they are crisp and golden. Drain the fried potatoes on kitchen paper.

Seakale

Seakale is one of the most exquisite of winter vegetables but unfortunately it is not often found in the greengrocer's shop and is more a prerogative of those who grow vegetables. If you can get hold of seakale, seize the opportunity; it has a flavour of asparagus and is delicious as it is a blanched vegetable and the shoots are picked when they are really tender.

Trim off the end of the seakale stalk, wash in lightly salted water and cook the stems exactly like asparagus, tied in bundles. Serve the stalks with melted butter of a hollandaise sauce.

The stalks can also be steamed or cooked in a little stock but care must be taken not to overcook as this will toughen them. They can also be cooked, drained, covered with a cheese sauce (see page 99), sprinkled with cheese and the dish browned under a hot grill.

Spinach

There are a number of leafed vegetables which go under the name of spinach but the true summer spinach has the best flavour and the greatest tenderness of all. Other leaves cooked and used in the same way include spinach beet, New Zealand spinach, Good King Henry and Swiss chard.

When very young spinach can be used as a delicious salad ingredient and when cooked it is essential that any form of spinach-type vegetables are only cooked as little as possible so that both their flavour and their goodness are retained.

Spinach weighs light but shrinks enormously while cooking so bear this in mind when you are buying the fresh vegetable – allow 2 lb of fresh spinach for four servings. It needs really good washing as the leaves seem to attract grit and soil from the garden. There used to be a saying that you should wash your spinach in seven changes of water but I must admit I find it easier just to wash it under plenty of running water. Pick over the spinach before washing, pulling off any tough stalks and discarding any discoloured leaves.

Having washed and dried your spinach, pack it in a large saucepan without any water (the water still sticking to the leaves will be enough liquid) and cook over a high heat, stirring every now and then until the leaves are just tender; this will only take a few minutes. Drain off any water that has come from the leaves, pressing them to get rid of as much liquid as possible.

Spinach can also be fried in a large frying pan. Wash and dry the spinach well and add 2 lb spinach to 2 tablespoons oil and 1 oz butter, cooking over a medium high heat, stirring frequently and seasoning with salt, freshly ground black pepper and adding a little lemon juice and perhaps a little ground nutmeg.

If cooked spinach is required for a dish, refresh the spinach under cold running water and drain it really well before using it as the method of the recipe demands. (Place your spinach in a colander or sieve and press it with the palms of your hands to squeeze out all possible excess water.)

Spinach purée

Serves 4
2 lb spinach
½ oz butter
4 tablespoons double cream
salt and freshly ground black pepper
pinch ground nutmeg

Trim, wash and cook the spinach as above. Drain really well. Combine the spinach and cream, and purée through a food mill or in a food processor. Melt the butter in a saucepan, add the spinach and season with salt, freshly ground black pepper and a little ground nutmeg and mix over a medium heat until the butter has been absorbed and the spinach is hot through.

Salads

What would summer foods be without salads, yet not much more than a hundred years ago salads were very much the exception rather than the rule and tomatoes were only ever served cooked. Now salads themselves are often served as a main course and, with the emphasis very much on slimming these days, the low calorie content of these dishes plays a great role in our diet.

On hot days the last thing one wants to do is to spend too much time in the kitchen so salads can be the perfect answer when you want to serve something that takes only a short time to prepare and needs no cooking. Nevertheless a good salad does need care taken over it; it must be absolutely fresh and the appearance of the dish must be attractive.

Buying and choosing salad ingredients
The majority of salad ingredients do not keep well for any length of time and should be bought fresh whenever possible. Most greengrocers get their fresh ingredients on Tuesdays, Wednesdays, Thursdays and Fridays and you will often find lettuces and other salad greens on sale on a Monday and Saturday are leftover, stale and limp.

Keep salad ingredients in a cool place or in a special container in the bottom of a refrigerator and make sure any bruised or spoilt leaves are removed before storing.

Wash salad ingredients as little as possible and always in cold water; a little salt added to the water will encourage any insects to remove themselves from the leaves.

Assembling mixed salads

Wash salads and dry them well before combining them in a large bowl. Wooden salad bowls are often used specially for salads and crushed clove of garlic is often rubbed around the bowl and the dressing then made in the bowl before the salad is added. Wooden bowls kept especially for this purpose should not be washed out but merely wiped with a soft cloth or some kitchen paper.

Salad dressings should not be added until the very last minute except with a few exceptions as, once the dressing has been added, salads quickly tend to go limp. Once lettuce has been dressed it cannot be kept and served a second time.

Toss salads very lightly to mix in the dressing just before serving. Attractive salads can be made by arranging different ingredients in stripes or circles and a dressing served separately. Different textures can be incorporated into salads by slicing some ingredients, shredding others and grating the harder ingredients like carrots, raw beetroot or cheese etc.

The basic vinaigrette dressing is made by combining oil, vinegar and seasonings but there are a great many variations which add both flavour and interest to a salad.

Using salad ingredients as a garnish

Salad ingredients used as garnishing material can add colour to summer foods. Use lettuce leaves, whole or shredded, as a bed or surround for cold food. Decorate dishes with slices of tomato, cucumber or radish. Use chopped hard-boiled egg whites and the yolks rubbed through a coarse sieve to sprinkle over cold mousses, cottage cheese salads and other cold ingredients. Finely chop celery leaves to sprinkle over hot or cold soups.

Salads as a first course

Out of the vast range of salad dishes there are many which make good first courses for either summer or winter eating. Salade Niçoise for instance, a mixture of crisp lettuce, tuna fish, cooked French beans, black olives, hard-boiled eggs and anchovies, makes an excellent starter as well as a main summer dish. A butter or kidney bean salad with tuna fish, olives and rings of raw onion served with a vinaigrette dressing provides a fairly filling dish before a light main course; egg mayonnaise can be as simple or as sophisticated as you wish and leeks or mushrooms *à la Greque* (cooked and dressed with a well-flavoured vinaigrette) are a good way to begin a meal at any time of the year. In France, during the summer, *crudités* (raw vegetable and salad ingredients carefully prepared and presented and served with a mayonnaise flavoured strongly with garlic) make a pleasant and sophisticated starter.

Salads as a main course

In the summer months when appetites are not quite so eager as they are in the winter, salads make the perfect alternative to a hot main course. The ingredients can be simple and the time involved in preparation cut to a minimum but the essential thing about these main course salads is their appearance. They must be attractive and colourful to look at and the ingredients must always be crisply fresh and never wilted or discoloured. Prepare main course salads shortly before you plan to serve them, garnish them prettily and allow enough time for chilling before serving them. Add the dressing at the last moment.

Basic salad ingredients and their preparation and storage

Bacon Crisply fried thin rashers of streaky bacon, drained on kitchen paper and crumbled can add flavour and interest to any number of salads. Add it to potato salads, rice salads, mixed green salads or young spinach salad.

Bean shoots Many supermarkets now sell these crisp white shoots which make a useful salad ingredient. Combine the shoots with grated raw carrot and dress with vinaigrette. Store in a polythene bag in the bottom of the refrigerator.

Beetroot Beetroot is usually bought ready cooked. It must be peeled and can then be cut into slices and dressed with vinegar to serve as a separate salad, sliced and added to mixed salads or diced and added to other ingredients that are to be dressed with mayonnaise. Raw beetroot can be grated and used as a delicious salad ingredient.

The juice of beetroot runs as soon as the root is peeled so any salad incorporating it will immediately become a rosy pink. Keep beetroot in a sealed container in the refrigerator. Uncooked beetroot should be washed and cooked with the skin left on for an hour or more until tender. Drain, cool and slide off the skin when the beetroot is cold. Small beetroot can be served whole with a little vinegar.

Cabbage, white and red In the winter months when salad ingredients are scarce, both white and red cabbage can be used to replace lettuce. Use really firm cabbage, the best of all are the white drumhead cabbages imported from Holland, and very finely slice through the leaves so that the cabbage is finely shredded. Remove any tough core before slicing. White cabbage is used as the base of a coleslaw salad which goes especially well with cold meat and ham.

Cabbage, when cut, tends to have a somewhat strong flavour and, except when a dressing is added to the cabbage and it is left to stand for a time before being served, it is best to shred the cabbage at the last possible moment before serving it.

Celeriac Here you have the texture of a root vegetable with the flavouring of celery. Don't be put off by the ugliness of this vegetable; its flavour is delicious and it can do great things for your salads. Once the root is peeled and cut it must be covered by cold water to which a teaspoon or two of lemon juice has been added. Prepared celeriac can be blanched (put into boiling water) for 2–3 minutes and then drained and left to cool before being used. Celeriac to be used for salads is usually cut into thin matchstick strips.

Celery Once celery was very much a winter vegetable and salad ingredient but now, with the introduction of new varieties, it is usually possible to buy it all the year round and this crisp crunchy vegetable adds greatly to mixed and main course salads. Cut off the base of the celery and divide into stalks. Trim off the tough leaves and any string from the tougher outer stalks and cut the stems into thin slices or sticks. The larger celery stalks are sometime stuffed with a cream or other soft cheese mixture. As a garnish, short lengths of celery stalks can be carefully cut into matchstick thick lengths three quarters of the way down the stalk and then covered with ice cold water so that the tops curl. The tender leaves from the heart of the celery can be chopped and added to mixed salads or used as a garnish for cold soups and other cold dishes. Crisp celery stalks also make a good accompaniment for cheese. Store whole celery in a polythene bag in the refrigerator. Stand trimmed celery stalks in a jar of cold water.

Cooked vegetables Cooked diced potatoes or carrots, peas, French beans or peeled broad beans can make acceptable salad ingredients.

Leeks, cooked, well drained and dressed when still warm, make a good salad dish or can be served as a first course.

Cubes of crisply fried bread Another unusual salad ingredient which is popular in America. Small cubes of white bread are crisply fried in lard or bacon fat and then well drained on kitchen paper. Added to other salad ingredients these supply a contrasting crisp crunchiness that is very good indeed.

Cucumber Cucumber, one of the coolest of all summer ingredients, contains a high percentage of water. If they are not to be used immediately, cucumber slices should be sprinkled with a little salt, left to stand for 20–30 minutes and then drained and the slices patted dry with kitchen paper – this is particularly necessary when the slices are to be used for garnishing something like a piece of salmon. Cucumber peel is usually removed before the cucumber is sliced but an attractive effect can be obtained by leaving thin strips of rind on the cucumber before slicing. Cucumber cut into half, lengthwise, with the peel removed and the seeds scooped out can be stuffed with other salad ingredients. Always slice cucumber from the flower not the stalk end and remove the peel with a potato peeler. Very thin slices can be obtained by slicing the cucumber through the wide blade of a grater or through a mandoline. Peeled, grated cucumber is added to cold soups and to some sauces. Thinly sliced cucumber sprinkled with vinegar makes a good accompaniment to cold fish and other summer dishes. Store cucumber in the salad container in the bottom of the refrigerator.

Fish salads Cold lobster, crab and prawns all make delicious centrepieces for a dish of salad as do a piece of cold salmon and smoked trout or mackerel. Serve the fish with quarters of lemon and a rich mayonnaise. Cooked white fish can also be incorporated and is especially good in a pasta salad.

Hard-boiled eggs for salads See page 103 in the section on eggs.

Herbs Herbs, although they should be used with a light hand, can add a great variety of flavours to salads. Chopped chives for instance give a mild onion flavour, garlic is often incorporated into salad dressings or into mayonnaise, chopped chervil gives a faintly peppery taste to other ingredients, fresh basil is delicious with tomatoes and finely chopped sorrel gives a fresh sharpness to a mixed salad. Finely chopped herbs are often added to dressings and salad sauces.

Lettuce The range of lettuces available all the year round is amazing. Don't be afraid to try out varieties you may never have seen before restricting yourself to the rather boring, uniform hot house lettuce that tends to be limp and tasteless. Try out the curly crinkled Webb's Wonder, the Long Cos, the slightly bitter endives and the crisply crunchy Arctic King. Combine different lettuces together in a salad bowl to give a variety of both taste and texture. Look out for the large Chinese cabbage lettuces which keep well and for Lamb's lettuce or corn salad which will add an interesting bittersweet flavour to your mixed salads.

If you have to keep lettuce for a day or two you will find that some keep better if they are washed, dried and packed in sealed polythene bags in the bottom of the refrigerator; others will maintain their freshness for longer if they are left whole, with any damaged leaves removed, before being put into an airtight container and stored in a cool dark place or in a special container in the bottom of the refrigerator.

Lettuces should be washed as little as possible and always dried well before storing. There are a number of commercial lettuce drying gadgets on the market which whizz the leaves around, spinning off any drops of water, and some of these are well worth buying if you plan to use a lot of lettuce during the year. Simpler methods are to place the washed leaves in a wire basket, colander or sieve and merely shake them vigorously to remove the excess water or to place the leaves in a clean tea towel, wrap it up loosely and swing the cloth to and fro until the water has been absorbed by the cloth. The best part of the lettuce is the heart and when you are buying these plants don't be afraid to part the outer leaves gently and see just what is in the centre. Forced lettuces have little heart and with these or rather tougher plants it is best to shred the leaves. Use your fingers for this purpose rather than a knife which tends to discolour and soften the leaves.

Most lettuces do not have much flavour themselves and need the additional accompaniment of a vinaigrette or other dressing, or mayonnaise, but the whole or shredded leaves can well be used as an attractive garnish for other salads. A bed of shredded lettuce for instance makes the perfect background for a mayonnaise salad of anything from hard-boiled eggs to chicken.

If you do find your lettuce gets limp there are some lovely old-fashioned tricks to help crisp them up. Lettuce put with a piece of cole into an old biscuit tin with a tightly fitting lid will crispen up overnight and so will the leaves if they are put into a bowl of water with ice cubes added to make it icy cold.

Meat and poultry Cold beef, pork, tongue, ham and poultry can all be used as the basis of a main course salad. Thinly slice the meat and arrange it on a plate surrounded with mixed salad ingredients. Beef or tongue can be cut into thin strips and combined with other ingredients in a vinaigrette dressing and chopped chicken or ham can be mixed with other ingredients in a mayonnaise. Chicken or ham can also be added to rice or pasta salad to serve as a first course. Lamb is not usually served cold but I personally think that thin slices of lamb that is slightly on the pink side served with mint sauce or redcurrant jelly and an interesting mixed salad can be delicious.

Pasta The idea of using pasta cold in a salad may seem a bit strange but in fact a good many forms of pasta, especially the shell shaped variety, makes a delicious base for a main course or side salad. Cook the pasta until tender in plenty of boiling salted water, rinse in cold water and drain well. Add some mayonnaise to the pasta while it is still warm and season generously with salt and freshly ground black pepper. For a main course salad add chopped chicken or ham, cooked peas, peeled and chopped tomatoes, finely chopped parsley and chives, tinned asparagus tips, crisply fried crumbled bacon, small cubes of peeled cucumber or finely chopped tinned pimento.

Peppers Peppers tend to confuse people so let me say at once that green, yellow and red peppers are all the same thing and not different varieties. The crisp green pepper is, like a tomato, an unripe fruit and the bright red or yellow, usually more expensive, fruit is merely ripened green produce. Both make delicious salad material. The peppery part of the fruit is the seeds in the centre and these, together with the whitish core, should always be removed before the pepper is served. Halve peppers and remove the stalks. Using a small sharp knife cut out the core and any seeds. Chop the flesh of the pepper or cut it into thin strips. Rings of pepper can be produced by cutting out the core and seeds from the stem end, leaving the fruit whole and cutting it into slices. Halved peppers, or whole pepper with a slice cut from the top and the core and seeds removed, make an attractive receptacle for mayonnaise salad mixtures. Chopped or thin strips of green or red peppers can be used as a garnish for cold dishes.

Radishes Radishes must be crisp. If they are not, forget them as their taste can be downright disgusting. Wash radishes as soon as they have been bought or pulled from the ground and either cut the tops off completely or leave about half an inch of stalk for holding the radish while you eat it. Cover the radishes with cold water and keep them in the refrigerator until required. Serve radishes in a small bowl on a bed of ice with drinks or slice them and add to mixed salads or to cold soups. Make radishes into fan shapes for decorating cold food by cutting them into thin slices almost all the way through from the stalk to the stem end; place the cut radishes into a bowl of iced water for 20 minutes and then fan out gently. As well as the ordinary round and long red radishes you will also find long white radishes the size of carrots on the market these days. They have a mild flavour and are very crisp.

Rice Rice makes an excellent replacement for a potato salad and can be served as either a main or a side dish. Cook long grain rice until tender and rinse in cold water. Drain well and mix in a vinaigrette dressing while the rice is still warm. Leave to cool and then mix in other chopped ingredients. You can add chopped chicken or ham, crisply fried and crumbled bacon, finely chopped chives and parsley, cooked peas, chopped green or red peppers or tinned pimento, peeled and chopped tomatoes, chopped celery or small cubes of peeled cucumber. Season the salad generously with salt and freshly ground black pepper.

Root vegetables Carrot, peeled and grated, gives a colourful touch and a good crunchy taste to mixed salads and, in the winter, try a little grated raw swede or turnip. Cooked new potatoes make some of the best summer salads ever. Cook the potatoes in their skins, peel them as soon as they are cool enough to handle, cut them into dice or slices and dress them with a French dressing or mayonnaise while they are still warm. Finely chopped chives or mint can be added to the salad.

Spinach In the early spring when the first young spinach appears the leaves make a good substitute for expensive lettuces. Wash and dry the leaves, shred them if necessary and use as lettuce. A very good salad can be made by combining spinach leaves with thinly sliced raw firm button mushrooms and crisply fried bacon. Toss the salad with a French dressing.

Spring onions, scallions or chipples These slightly strong tasting young onions have a good flavour and, if you like the taste of onions, they can do a lot for a salad. Strip off the brown outer leaves from the bulbs and trim any brown or yellow tops from the green stems. The onions can be left whole or cut lengthwise into four. Sometimes the spring onions are finely chopped to use in potato and other salads or the green tops are finely chopped to use in the place of chives as a garnish for cold dishes. Store spring onions in a cool dark place or in the salad compartment of a refrigerator. If the onions are to be stored in the refrigerator they should be kept covered to prevent their smell affecting other produce.

Tinned ingredients used in salads Both butter beans in brine and red kidney beans make a good salad base. Drain and toss the beans in a French dressing and combine them with chopped chives, raw onion rings and finely chopped parsley.

Tinned fish can also be used as the base of a salad or as ingredients of a mixed salad. Tuna fish is especially versatile, anchovy fillets can be chopped or left whole, tinned salmon and crab can make the base of a main course salad and sardines can be used as part of a mixed salad plate. Tinned asparagus or artichoke hearts or bottoms make good salad ingredients and a tin of sweetcorn can also be incorporated into mixed salads. Tinned pimento, chopped or sliced, adds both colour and flavour to salad dishes and can be used as a garnish.

Tinned stringless French beans can be used in the place of fresh beans in the delicious Salade Niçoise.

Tomatoes Commercially grown tomatoes are usually picked when they are under-ripe and often need to be kept for a day or two before being used; ideally a tomato for salads should be firm but bright red in appearance with no yellow or even green patches. The stalk should come out easily and the inside of the fruit be brightly coloured without the slightly furry texture that indicates a prematurely picked fruit. Never buy too many tomatoes at one time. It is impossible sometimes to gauge flavour from appearance and a tomato that looks large ripe and bonny in a shop may, when you cut it in half, turn out to be tough and lacking in flavour.

Smell is a great indication of flavour and a perfectly ripe tomato will have a deliciously sweet and summery scent if sniffed around the stalk. Watch out for the large Mediterranean tomatoes being imported from the Continent. These are often ugly in shape but they have a good flavour and are especially good for cooking with. It is also sometimes possible to buy yellow or golden tomatoes which have a sweet flavour.

Keep unripe tomatoes on a sunny windowsill to ripen them. Store firm ripe tomatoes in a cool dark place or in the salad compartment at the bottom of a refrigerator.

To peel tomatoes Tomatoes that are to be used in a cooked dish or for salads and which have a slightly tough skin should be skinned. Cover the tomatoes with boiling water and leave them to stand for 1 minute. Drain well, pierce the skins lightly with a fork and slide them off.

Coring and de-seeding tomatoes Many cooked dishes using tomatoes require them to have the core and seeds removed before they are used. Quarter the skinned tomatoes and cut out the core with a sharp knife. Scoop out the seeds with a small teaspoon.

Slicing tomatoes Use a well-sharpened knife and slice the tomatoes from stalk end.

Stuffing tomatoes Both cold and hot stuffed tomatoes make an attractive and decorative dish. Cut a slice off the stalk end of the tomatoes and reserve the slice. Using a teaspoon or a grapefruit spoon with a sharp point scoop out the seeds and flesh of the tomato without breaking through the skin.

Decorative tomatoes Tomatoes cut into decorative shapes can be used to garnish cold food and salads. They are also used as a garnish for some hot dishes but I personally always feel this is something of a mistake. Either cut the tomatoes into thin slices to within a quarter of an inch of one side of the tomato so that the slices fan open, or cut around the side in a neat zig-zag pattern so that when the two halves are separated the halves have an attractive flower-like edge.

Watercress This slightly peppery salad ingredient is delicious in its own right as well as being a good mixer in a combination salad. Remove the tough stems and wash and dry the leaves before using. Watercress is used as a garnish for both hot and cold foods (it goes well with steak or grilled meat or chicken) and it is often dipped into a vinaigrette dressing before being used to decorate cold dishes.

Fruit and Puddings

Fruit

Fresh fruit is an essential part of a healthy diet but fruit also plays a major part in the making of sweets and puddings of all kinds. Always choose fruit that is firm, ripe and unblemished. When you are cutting fruit that discolours with contact to the air (bananas, apples, pears, peaches, nectarines etc.) brush the surface of the fruit with a little lemon juice as soon as it is cut – this will preserve the colour.

A fresh fruit bowl

There are few things more delicious as an ending to a simple meal than a bowl of fresh fruit and a selection of cheeses served with crisp biscuits and some crisp stalks of celery. Choose fruit in season, polish fruit with a shiny skin (apples, pears etc.) by rubbing the skin gently with a soft cloth and pile the fruit attractively in a shallow bowl. Small knives should be provided to peel fruit. Napkins are essential as some fruit is messy to prepare at the table and it's helpful to have a pair of scissors if grapes are to be included amongst the fruit.

Preparing fruit for puddings
Use a silver, silver plated or stainless steel knife for preparing all fruit.

Apples and pears Thinly peel the fruit, cut it into quarters and neatly cut out the core. Cut the quarter into thin slices and place into a bowl with the juice of a lemon in it as you prepare the slices. Make sure that all the slices are covered with lemon juice.

Bananas Choose firm bananas with no blemishes. Peel the fruit, cut it into thin slices and brush the slices with lemon juice as soon as they are cut. Bananas go mushy very quickly so these should be prepared at the last possible minute and not left with other ingredients in a mixed fruit salad.

Citrus fruits Peel oranges, tangerines and grapefruit etc., and either peel the segments or remove as much pith as possible from the outside of the peeled fruit and cut the fruit into thin slices. This, however, is only really suitable for thin skinned oranges as grapefruit and the tangerine family tend to have too much pith and too thick a skin for this preparation.

Strawberries, raspberries etc. Avoid washing these fruits unless it is absolutely necessary as contact with water tends to make the fruit mushy and to destroy its flavour. Hull the fruit and treat it gently so that the fruit does not break up or become squashed.

Currants As these tend to be rather a sharp fruit they are more often cooked than served raw. Top and tail the fruit before using them unless you are going to purée them through a food mill.

Peaches, nectarines and apricots Unless you are fortunate enough to buy nectarines with very thin skins these fruits usually need to be peeled before being used. Cover the fruit with boiling water, leave for 1 minute and then drain off the water. Slide off the peel and brush the fruit at once with lemon juice to prevent the flesh going brown.

Pineapple One of the great mistakes made when buying pineapples is to buy them over-ripe. The fruit *should* have a certain amount of green on its skin and not be, as most people seem to believe, golden all over to be fit to eat. Choose firm fruit with a sweet smell. Using a sharp knife cut away the skin of the fruit and with a potato peeler scoop out any pits of skin left after peeling. Cut the fruit into four lengthwise around the hard central core, and then cut it again into thin fingers about ½-inch thick and two inches long. For a mixed fruit salad the fruit can be cut into cubes but on the whole the flavour of this fruit is so distinctive that I think it is better to serve it by itself. For a spectacular sweet cut the unpeeled pineapple in half, carefully cut out the flesh from each half, remove the core and fill the pineapple halves with the cut dressed fruit or with pineapple ice cream.

Melon Halve the melon and scoop out the seeds, remove the skin and cut the flesh into wedge-shaped slices or scoop out the flesh with a melon scoop.

Cherries Cherries are delicious in a fruit salad. Wash them in cold water and dry them well. Remove the stems and push out the pips with a hairpin or with a special gadget which can be bought from kitchenware shops. Use white cherries for a pale coloured salad and the red or black cherries for a red fruit salad.

Plums The best plums for fruit salads are the large bright red or golden plums which are imported into this country in the spring and summer. Their skins tend to be firm but not too tough and they do not need to be peeled. Although their flavour can be rather sharp their texture is delicious in a mixed fruit salad. Cut the plums off their stones into thickish slices. Home grown plums should be peeled before being used as their skins are on the tough side. Drop the plums into boiling water, leave for 1 minute then drain and slide off the skins. Halve the plums, remove the stones and brush the cut plums with lemon juice to prevent them going brown.

Grapes The best grapes of all for a fruit salad are those small seedless ones which need no preparation at all other than removing the stalks. Large grapes will need to be halved and have their pips removed and, if their skins are tough, the skin should also be removed – a messy job but one well worth doing.

Fruit puddings

Most of the popular puddings are based on fruit. Fortunately there is fresh fruit on sale all the year round and so it makes sense to buy the fruit that is in season for using in your puddings. You can buy imported fruit that is out of season but usually it tends to be very expensive. The range of puddings that are based on fruit is very wide one but here are some ideas for preparing and cooking fruit for the most popular of these puddings.

Serving fresh fruit

Most fruit is improved by being served chilled; cover first before refrigerating.

Strawberries, raspberries, blackberries and loganberries

These make delicious puddings served uncooked with sugar and cream. Pick over the fruit (try not to wash it unless it is absolutely necessary) and remove the stalks if necessary. Put the fruit into a serving bowl, sprinkle generously with castor sugar, add a little lemon juice and leave to stand in a refrigerator for one hour before serving. Serve with whipped, double or clotted cream.

Melon

Melon is often served as a first course but it also (especially if the melons are ripe and sweet) makes a delicious pudding. Halve the melon if it is very small, scoop out the seeds and sprinkle the cavity with some castor sugar and a little lemon juice; cut larger melons in half, scoop out the seeds, and then cut them into thick slices and sprinkle with sugar and a little lemon juice. The centre of small melons can be filled with fresh fruit such as raspberries or blackberries or it can be filled with some port, fruit syrup or with a scoop of ice cream. Melon can also be served in individual glasses, cut into scoops with a ball-cutter – an attractive way of serving this is to combine the flesh of yellow and red melon. Balls of melon also go well in a fresh fruit salad.

Pineapple

Fresh pineapple makes a good ending to a rich meal. Choose a ripe pineapple, cut off the skin and either cut the flesh into slices or into finger-thick chunks. Cut out the core, sprinkle the fruit with castor sugar and, if you like, with a little kirsch.

Oranges

A delicious fresh pudding is made by peeling oranges, removing the white membrane, cutting the oranges in thin slices and discarding the pips. Arrange the slices in a shallow serving dish and sprinkle with castor sugar and, if you like, with a little kirsch. Cover the dish and refrigerate for at least three hours before serving.

Baked apples

Large cooking apples can be baked to make warming winter puddings. Choose even-sized apples, wash and core the fruit and cut a thin line around the middle of each apple to prevent them bursting. Stand apples in a baking dish and fill the centre with a mixture of brown sugar and cinnamon, top with a knob of butter and surround with $\frac{1}{4}$ inch of water. Bake the apples in a moderate oven

(350°F/180°C Reg. 4) for about 45 minutes. The apples can also be filled with a mixture of chopped nuts and dried fruit.

Stewed fruit

Apples, pears, plums, gooseberries, rhubarb and currants can all be stewed gently to make puddings which can be served hot or cold with cream or custard.

Prepare the fruit and combine it with some sugar and a little water in a heavy saucepan. Bring to the boil and then simmer gently until the fruit is tender. Serve hot or leave to cool and then refrigerate until cold.

Stewed dried fruit

Dried fruit should be soaked overnight in cold water (some people like to soak prunes in cold tea). Combine the fruit with some sugar and the water in which the fruit was soaked, bring to the boil and simmer gently until the fruit is tender. Serve hot or leave to cool and then refrigerate until cold. A strip of lemon and some cinnamon and cloves can be added to the fruit when it is cooking to give extra flavour.

Fruit fritters

Ripe firm fruit can be coated in a sweet batter and then deep-fried to make delicious sweet fritters. Thickly slice bananas; peel, core and slice cooking apples; slice pineapple or drain tinned pineapple. Fruit that is on the sour side should be left to stand with a sprinkling of sugar for an hour before using and patted dry with kitchen paper.

Use a batter that is lightened with the beaten white of an egg and deep-fry the fritters, a few at a time, in very hot cooking oil. Drain the fritters on kitchen paper and sprinkle with sugar before serving.

Fruit flans

Fruit flans can be made from almost any fruit. Strawberries, raspberries, loganberries, blackberries, bananas, tinned pineapple, tinned peaches and apricots can all be used raw but most other fruit will need to be cooked before being used as a filling for the flan.

Flan cases either made from pastry or from a sponge mixture, should be pre-cooked before adding the fruit and the fruit is then usually covered with a jelly and chilled before serving. A quick jelly for fruit flans can be made by melting redcurrant jelly and pouring it over the fruit.

Fresh fruit salad
One of the most popular puddings especially when served after a fairly heavy meal. Home-made fruit salads bear no relation to the synthetic fruit that comes out of a tin, although there may be times when you will want to add a little tinned fruit to a fresh fruit salad in order to stretch the ingredients.

There are two kinds of fruit salad, a plain variety that is made up of one, two or perhaps three varieties of fruit and those that contain a combination of a great many fruits. Fresh fruit is available all the year round these days and the enchantment of fruit salads is that you can alter their taste, colour and appearance with the seasons. You can get great variety into your fruit salads by considering with care the fruit you are going to include in them. A citrus salad, for instance, that combines oranges, clementines and some grapefruit segments can be very pleasant and so can a salad that contains only red fruit such as strawberries, cherries, plums and raspberries.

The fruit for these salads should be prepared with care not just chopped roughly and tossed in a bowl. All pips and cores must be removed, sliced fruit should be thinly and neatly cut and diced fruit should be uniform in size. Beware of making salads too sickly by adding too much sugar to your syrup. If the syrup is too sweet counteract this by adding some lemon juice which helps bring out the flavour of the fruit.

Fruits suitable for use in fruit salads Apples, pears (place slices of apples and pears into water to which some lemon juice has been added, immediately after peeling and slicing to prevent the flesh turning brown), grapes (peel and remove pips), melon, oranges, pineapple.

Making the Syrup for a fruit salad Most fruits contain a good deal of liquid in their own right and some of the best fruit salads are made by layering the prepared fruit with some castor or icing sugar, adding just a little wine, fresh orange juice or liquor and leaving the fruit to macerate for at least 24 hours in a cool place so that their juices are drawn out by the sugar. In this way you get the real fresh taste of the fruit without it being thinned by a syrup. Firm fruit that does need a sugar syrup should not be swamped by the liquid and the syrup should always have the addition of some lemon juice to give it extra flavour.

The amount of syrup you require and the strength it should be depends on the amount of fruit, and its own sweetness, that you are going to use. As a rough guide use twice as much water as sugar and heat through until the syrup comes to the boil and the sugar has dissolved. Syrups can be thickened with some arrowroot in which case the arrowroot should be mixed to a paste with a little water before being added to the syrup and stirred over a medium heat until the syrup has thickened and is clear and shining.

Fruit fools

These simple sweets can be made from either fresh or stewed fruit puréed and then combined with whipped cream.

Fresh fruit to use for fools Strawberries, raspberries, blackberries, loganberries and bananas. Purée the berries and then rub through a fine sieve to remove the pips before combining with sugar and whipped cream.

Fruit that should be cooked before being used Apples, pears, gooseberries, rhubarb and currants. Cook the fruit with a little water and sugar until it is tender and then purée it until smooth. Leave the fruit to cool before adding the cream.

Making the fool The usual proportion of fruit to cream is half and half, although a less extravagant sweet is made by using half cream and half custard. The cream is whipped until thick and then the prepared sweetened fruit is lightly folded into the cream. The sweet is piled into a bowl or individual glasses and chilled before serving.

Fruit tarts or pies

Most fruit tarts or pies are made with a rich shortcrust pastry. The tarts or pies can be made with cooked or raw fruit, sweetened with sugar and with either a pastry case and topping or just a topping.

Suitable fruits Rhubarb, currants, blackberries, apples, pears, plums and cherries.

To make the pie Roll out the pastry and, if a double shelled pie is required, line a pie dish or pie plate with half the pastry. Prepare the fruit for cooking (i.e. peel, core and stone as necessary). Lightly stew the fruit if necessary.

If using raw fruit place three-quarters of the fruit in the pie dish, add enough sugar to sweeten and then cover with the remaining fruit. Cut a thin strip of pastry to go round the pie dish, damp the edge so that the pastry will stick firmly to the dish and top with the pastry topping. Seal the edges firmly and cut an air vent in the centre. The pastry topping can be brushed with beaten egg or milk and sprinkled with sugar before baking or half way through the cooking time to give a good golden brown crust.

Fruit pancakes
Puréed fruit makes a good filling for pancakes.

Cold fruit soufflés or mousses
Made with a base of egg yolks, whipped with sugar, fruit purée (and occasionally with chunks of fruit added), gelatine, egg whites and whipped cream.

Puddings

Many puddings are variations on a basic theme. Once you know how to make one basic pudding you can adapt the recipe to many other flavours.

Gelatine is used in many cold sweets and puddings but should be used with care since too little will lead to the pudding not being properly set and too much will give it an unpleasant taste and texture. $\frac{1}{2}$ oz (1 tablespoon) or 1 packet gelatine is usually enough to set 1 pint of ingredients although slightly more may have to be used in warm weather. Soak the gelatine in warm water until the crystals are dissolved before adding the gelatine mixture to the other ingredients. The basic ingredients, including the gelatine mixture, are usually left until they are beginning to set before the cream or whipped egg whites are folded in.

Bread and butter pudding
An inexpensive pudding using up stale pieces of bread. It usually has a custard base.

Charlottes
Stewed fruit which is baked in a mould lined with slices of buttered or fried bread.

Christmas pudding
Should be made a few months before Christmas and the richer it is the better it will keep. Store Christmas puddings in an airtight container.

Custards
Although custard is often served as an accompaniment to a pudding there are many variations on the custard theme which make excellent puddings in their own right. The simplest of these is a baked custard made with egg yolks, milk, sugar and a flavouring of vanilla. Other custards are flavoured with chocolate or, in the case of *crême caramel* with a caramel coating.

Flambé puddings

Bananas and cherries make good flambé puddings to serve on a special occasion. Peel bananas and cut them into half lengthwise, cook them in butter until soft, add sugar and some orange and lemon juice, pour over 2 tablespoons of brandy, bring to the boil and when the ingredients are bubbling, set light to the liquid which will burn with a blue flame. 'Cherries Jubilee', black cherries in syrup, is made the same way with the cherries being served on top of vanilla ice cream.

Jellies

Fruit jellies Although you can buy commercial fruit jellies a much better flavour is achieved by using fresh fruits. Fruits suitable to use for jellies are lemons, oranges, currants, raspberries and strawberries. Cook the fruit if necessary and squeeze out the juice by rubbing the fruit through a very fine sieve. Add enough gelatine to set the jelly and chill in a refrigerator until set.

Milk jellies Milk can be added to jellies to give them extra body. Cool the jelly and add half the amount of cold milk to the amount of jelly.

Junket

Made by adding rennet to warm milk and leaving to set. The junket can be flavoured with rum or brandy and can be topped with flakes of chocolate or with grated nutmeg.

Meringue puddings

Meringue can be used as a topping, made into a base for fruit (a pavlova) or into meringue baskets for containing fresh or stewed fruit.

Milk puddings

Milk puddings are made from short grain rice, tapioca or semolina. Soak the grains in milk before using and cook the pudding in a slow oven (300°F/150°C Reg. 2) stirring it once or twice during the cooking time to distribute the grains throughout the pudding.

Pancakes

Traditionally pancakes are served with lemon juice and sprinkled with sugar but more exotic pancakes can be made by filling with puréed fruit.

Soufflés

There are both hot and cold pudding soufflés. Hot soufflés are made in the same way as savoury ones with a basis of butter, flour, egg yolks, flavouring (i.e. lemon jusice and rind, chocolate, rum, Grand Marnier etc.) and stiffly beaten egg whites. Cold soufflés are made with egg yolk, sugar, flavouring and gelatine base with stiffly beaten egg whites and whipped cream folded into the basic ingredients.

Steamed puddings
These are ideal to serve when the weather is cold but, since they are inclined to be a little heavy and rich, they should not be served after too heavy a main course. Steamed puddings are either made with a sponge or a suet mixture basis and they are usually flavoured with fruit, jams, golden syrup, chocolate or with dried fruit.

Syllabubs
Light sweets of double cream whipped until stiff with a flavouring folded into it. The classic syllabub is made with lemon juice and sherry but you can also use the same principle with other fruit purée or juice flavourings.

Tarts
There are a large variety of open fruit tarts to choose from but tarts are also filled with custard, a treacle mixture and many other ingredients. The pastry shell is usually partially or wholly baked before the filling is added.

Trifle
One of the most popular of all British puddings. Sponge cake is soaked in a little sherry and topped with some fruit and jam. Custard is put in a thick layer over the fruit and left to set. The trifle is decorated with for example whipped cream and glacé cherries. A layer of jelly can also be added above the fruit.

Stocks and Soups

Although the twentieth century has brought one of those most useful of aids, the stock cube, into our kitchens we have also lost a lot by tending to lose sight of the good old-fashioned stock pot and those useful Victorian flavouring additives of mushroom ketchup, anchovy essence and Harvey's sauce. Stock cubes are invaluable for adding extra flavour or for use in any emergency but please don't overlook the rewards of stock-making especially if you have a deep freeze; stocks make valuable use of ingredients you might otherwise throw away, they are full of goodness and nourishment, reasonably inexpensive to make and, if you like the good things in life, they have an individual flavour you just cannot imitate with commercial products. Stocks that need a long cooking time can quickly be made in a pressure cooker and a good store of stock in your freezer gives you the base of any number of very valuable dishes.

General guidelines for making stocks

Colour is important so brown ingredients for a rich brown stock to give a good colour before adding the liquid. Do not allow ingredients to brown if you are making a white stock.

Add plenty of vegetables to your main ingredients to give a good flavour. Do not however add strong-flavoured vegetables, i.e. cabbage or potatoes. Use fresh herbs when possible for flavouring and season your stocks generously.

Strain stocks through a sieve lined with muslin to get rid of all the impurities. Muslin can be bought reasonably inexpensively and can be washed and used again and again.

If the flavour of your stock is not quite strong enough it can be intensified by boiling the stock to reduce it, or by the addition of a stock cube.

Extra colour can be added by incorporating onion and tomato skins and mushroom peelings into your basic ingredients. You can also boil some shin beef in the stock to enrich it, using the boiled meat afterwards as the basis of a minced meat dish.

Almost any stock you make will contain fat. Pour the stock into a wide bowl after straining, leave to cool and then chill in a refrigerator until the fat has formed a skin across the surface of the stock. Carefully lift off the set fat before using the stock. If you are in a hurry you can soak up this fat by gently pressing a layer of kitchen paper across the surface.

For clear soups stocks will need to be clarified, a process which is not as professional and complicated as it sometimes sounds and which can easily be done at home. See details for the clarification of stocks in the recipe for Consommé.

Follow the instructions in your pressure cooking manual for making stocks in the pressure cooker.

Stocks and their uses

Basic meat stock
A brown stock should be rich in colour and full of flavour. Basic meat stock can be used as the base of a consommé or for any meat or vegetable soups that do not require a white stock. Basic meat stock is also used for sauces and for adding to stews and casseroles.

Vegetable stock
A white stock made by simmering a combination of vegetables. Use for vegetable soups and purées to give additional flavour and as a less expensive addition to stews and casseroles in the place of a meat stock.

Chicken and veal stock
White stocks that are used as a base for soups and sauces.

Stock from cooked carcasses

There is a lot of flavour left in the carcass of chicken, duck or turkey etc. after it has been roasted and served. Don't throw away a carcass but simmer it with vegetables and herbs to make a nourishing stock base for soups, sauces and for adding to stews and casseroles.

Fish stock

Always ask your fishmonger for the heads, tails and trimmings of filleted fish. You pay for the whole fish when you buy it so don't be cheated out of the valuable trimmings that can be simmered with vegetables and herbs to make an excellent cooking liquid for poached fish, as the base of a fish soup and as flavouring ingredient for sauces to serve with fish.

Steps to stock-making

1. Prepare the vegetables and other ingredients in a large, heavy pan that has a tight-fitting lid. Cover the ingredients with cold water, add herbs and season generously.
2. Bring the liquid slowly to the boil skimming off any scum that rises to the surface with a perforated spoon.
3. Cover tightly and simmer over a low heat (this can be done inside a solid fuel stove) for 2–3 hours.
4. Strain the stock through a sieve lined with a double piece of muslin (you can use a hair sieve but muslin is best and it can be used again and again). Leave the stock to cool in a large bowl, refrigerate when cold and leave until the fat has formed a skin over the surface of the stock.
5. To concentrate the stock, return it to a clean pan and bring to the boil. Boil the stock over a high heat until it is reduced to the required intensity of flavour.
6. Store stock in the refrigerator. Meat stock can be kept for up to four days, vegetable stock will need to be brought to the boil each day and fish stock should be used within 24 hours of making.

Basic meat stock

Shin beef provides the full-bodied flavour of this stock. You can use the shin, minced, for a left-over meat dish as shepherd's pie.

Ask your butcher to chop up the bones for you.

Makes 3 pints stock.

1 lb shin beef

2 lb beef bones (preferably marrow bones)

4 pints water
2 carrots
1 onion
6 peppercorns
½ teaspoon salt
1 stick celery
4 sprigs parsley
2 bay leaves

Place the bones in a roasting pan and roast them in a hot (450°F/240°C Reg 8) for about 15 minutes until the bones are browning. Drain off and reserve the fat in the pan. Place the bones and meat in a large heavy-bottomed saucepan, pour over the water, add the peppercorns and salt, bring to the boil, lower the heat, cover and simmer gently for two hours.

Scrub and roughly chop the carrot. Wash the onion but leave on the outer skin. Roughly chop the onion and the celery. Heat the fat from the bones in a saucepan. Add the vegetables to the fat and cook them over a medium heat, stirring to prevent sticking, until the onions are coloured and the fat has been absorbed. Add the vegetables to the stock with the parsley and bay leaves, return to the boil, lower the heat, cover and simmer for a further hour.

Strain the stock into a large bowl through a sieve lined with muslin and leave to cool. Refrigerate until the fat has formed a firm layer over the surface (if you are in a hurry you can soak up the fat with absorbent kitchen paper). Remove the fat.

Use for soups, stews and casseroles and add as much stock as is required in the recipe.

To make consommé

For consommés the meat strained stock is boiled to intensify the flavour and then clarified to produce a beautiful clear, aromatic and richly bodied soup which can also be used as an aspic jelly with the addition of gelatine crystals (the stock will jelly by itself but for aspic you need a little extra setting strength, see Aspic on page 1).

Serves 4–5

3 pints basic meat stock
1 egg white
egg shell
juice of ½ lemon
4 tablespoons sherry

Put the stock into a clean saucepan, bring to the boil and boil over a high heat until the liquid is reduced by one-third (it is sometimes confusing to measure stock when it is boiling so measure 2 pints into your saucepan, mark the level with a waterproof pen and then boil the stock until the mark is just uncovered).

Beat the egg white until just stiffening. Break the eggshell into small pieces. Add the egg shell and egg white to the stock and bring slowly back to the boil, lightly whisking the egg white and shell into the stock using a wire or rotary whisk. Boil for three minutes without whisking, remove from the heat and leave for the froth to subside. Return the saucepan to the heat, bring back to the boil once more and remove and leave to settle. Strain through a double thickness of muslin. By this time the stock should be absolutely clear and a rich amber colour. If the stock is not clear, repeat the clarifying process by using a second egg white and shell.

Return the clarified consommé to a clean pan, add the lemon juice and sherry, check seasoning, bring to the boil and serve very hot.

Cold consommé
Leave the consommé to cool and then refrigerate until set and well chilled. Break up the consommé with a fork, divide amongst soup bowls and serve very well chilled with a garnish of thin half lemon slices.

Consommé with tomato
Add 1½ tablespoons tomato purée to the stock before clarifying. Serve hot or cold.

Alternative garnishes for consommé
1. Add Madeira in the place of the sherry for a richer flavour.
2. Make two pancakes (see page 117) and leave them to cool. Roll the pancakes up tightly and cut them into very thin slices. Float the resulting strips of pancakes in the consommé just before serving.
3. Drain a small tin of tuna fish of all its oil. Lightly break up the fish with a fork and float the flakes of tuna in the consommé.
4. Add very thin strips of lean tongue or ham to the finished consommé.

Chicken stock
1 chicken carcass (and giblets)
3 pints water
1 chicken stock cube
2 carrots

1 large onion
2 sticks celery
2 sprigs parsley
2 bay leaves
pinch of salt
8 white peppercorns

Break up the chicken carcass and put it into a large heavy saucepan with the herbs. Wash, but do not peel the onion and cut it into quarters. Peel and roughly chop the carrot and the sticks of celery leaving the leaves on. Add the vegetables, stock cube, salt and pepper to the chicken (and the giblets), cover with cold water, bring to the boil, cover tightly and simmer for two hours.

Strain the stock into a bowl through a sieve lined with muslin leave to cool and refrigerate until the fat has formed a skin over the surface. Skim off the skin.

Chicken consommé can be made in the same way as Consommé see page 66 and is deliciously light and nourishing served either hot or cold with a little lemon juice and perhaps a little dry sherry.

Stock from a carcass

1 large cooked chicken, duck or turkey carcass
1 large onion
1 stock cube
3 carrots
2 sticks celery
1 strip lemon peel
2 sprigs parsley
2 bay leaves
salt and freshly ground black pepper

Break up the carcass and put it into a large heavy pan. Wash the onion, leave the skin on and cut the onion into quarters. Scrub and roughly chop the carrots. Roughly chop the celery leaving the leaves on. Add the vegetables to the carcass with the lemon peel, herbs and stock cube. Season with salt and pepper. Cover the ingredients completely with cold water, bring slowly to the boil, skim off any scum that rises to the surface, cover tightly and simmer over a low heat, so that the water is only just moving, for two hours. Strain the stock through a fine sieve or a sieve lined with muslin and leave to cool. Refrigerate the cooled stock until the skin forms a solid skin across the surface. Remove the skin and use the stock as a base for soups or to make gravy or add to stews and casseroles etc.; or serve it as a soup with the addition of some finely chopped cooked turkey, chicken etc.

Vegetable stock

A lightly flavoured stock can be made with vegetables and it is always worth saving the liquid in which vegetables that have a not too strong taste have been cooked to incorporate into your home-made stocks. A vegetable stock makes a very good alternative to plain water when making a vegetable soup adding both flavour and body to the soup.

3 carrots
2 large onions
2 tomatoes
2 sticks celery
1 small turnip
1 stock cube
3 pints water
salt and pepper
2 bay leaves
3 sprigs parsley

Wash, but do not peel, and then roughly chop the carrots and onion. Quarter the tomatoes. Roughly chop the celery leaving the leaves on. Peel and roughly chop the turnip. Combine the vegetables in a large heavy saucepan, add the herbs and stock cube, season with salt and pepper, cover with the cold water, bring to the boil, cover tightly and simmer for 1½ hours. Strain the stock through a fine sieve.

Note Extra flavour can be gained by sautéing the vegetables very gently in a little dripping before adding the herbs etc. Use only about ½ oz dripping as the fat must be completely absorbed by the vegetables before the other ingredients are added.

General guidelines to the making of soups

Soups make a marvellous form of food for almost any occasion. They are not only one of the perfect ways to start a meal but can also be served as a main course in their own right. Soups are popular with all the family, economical and nourishing; they can be quickly made out of often the most humble of ingredients, many soups can be made in advance and this form of food makes a very good centre course of informal buffet parties. Soups can be served hot or cold and provide what is perhaps the most colourful range of dishes for the home cook.

Points to watch when making soups

1. Soups must be well flavoured and well coloured. Increase flavour by adding a stock cube to a light stock, tomato purée, herbs or spices to add body, careful and imaginative seasoning to add interest and a good garnishing to provide both colour and sophistication to the finished dish.
2. In vegetable and most meat soups the ingredients should be evenly and finely chopped to provide the right texture.
3. A good stock is essential as the base for almost all soups; use home-made stocks when possible (see Stocks, page 165).
4. All fat must be skimmed from the surface of the soup before it is to be served – if necessary cool and refrigerate the finished soup until the fat has formed a firm skin over the surface, skim off the fat before re-heating. A small amount of fat can be absorbed by floating a piece of absorbent kitchen paper over the surface of the hot soup.
5. Hot soups must be served really hot cold soups really well chilled. Heat soup bowls for hot liquids and, if possible, chill those in which a cold soup is to be served. Cold soups can be given an extra chill by having an ice cube or two added to the soup when it is brought to the table but remember that this will tend to dilute the flavour a little.
6. Puréed soups should be absolutely smooth. Purée vegetables etc. through the fine blades of a food mill, in an electric liquidiser or in a food processor.
7. Thickened soups must be free from the taste of the thickening agent. Soups are thickened by the addition of flour, or in some cases cornflour, or by adding egg yolks or cream. Once egg yolks or cream have been beaten into the soup it must not be allowed to boil or the liquid will separate and curdle.
8. The fish in fish soups must never be allowed to overcook or it will toughen. Most fish soups need very little cooking.

Garnishes for soups

Add garnishings at the very last minute before serving.

Hot soups Finely chopped parsley, chervil, chives or celery leaves. A little grated carrot. Thin slices of lemon or orange with the pips removed. Croutons of crisply fried bread (cut white bread with the crusts removed into very small cubes and fry until crisp and golden brown, drain off excess fat on kitchen paper and serve the croutons in a separate bowl). Crumbled, crisply fried bacon (fry streaky bacon rashers until very crisp; drain on kitchen paper, remove the rind and crumble the bacon into small pieces). Spoonfuls of sour cream.

Cold soups Finely chopped chives or celery leaves. Thin slices of lemon or orange with the pips removed. Spoonfuls of sour cream (1 spoonful for each serving). Finely shredded lettuce leaves. Peeled tomato with the core and seeds removed and the flesh very finely chopped. Finely chopped green pepper.

Cream soups

Rich, velvety soups usually suitable for cold weather evenings. The thickness and smoothness can be obtained by adding flour and milk to the purėed soup, by beating in a mixture of softened butter and flour or by the addition of cream or beaten egg yolks. Chicken, vegetables and sometimes fish are used as a basis for these soups.

Thickening cream soup

Flour or other cereals The flour is added after the main ingredients have been cooked and purėed. Mix the flour to a smooth paste with milk or other liquid. Add a little of the flour mixture to the soup, stirring well and gradually blending in the rest. Bring to the boil and boil for at least three minutes until the soup has thickened and any taste of raw flour has gone.

Mixture of flour and butter This is technically referred to as a thickening of *beurre manie* and gives the soup a richer, more shining appearance.

Mix 1 oz softened butter with 2 tablespoons flour until you get a smooth soft paste. Add a little of the paste to the boiling vegetable purée and whisk it in with a wire whisk. Continue adding the paste, a little at a time and whisking it in well, until you get the required thickness of the soup.

Cream Add the cream to hot but not boiling soup, whisk it in well and re-heat the soup without boiling.

Egg yolks Beat 2 egg yolks with 4 tablespoons cream or milk. Add a few spoonfuls of the hot soup and mix well. Gradually add this mixture to the soup stirring vigorously all the time. Do not boil the soup once the yolks have been added.

Achieving the ideal consistency in cream soups
If a cream soup is too thick (it should be the consistency of thin cream) thin it by adding additional stock or milk. If the soup is too thin or the flavour on the weak side it can be thickened by being reduced at the purée stage by boiling the purée over a high heat without covering. Cream soups can be cooked in advance and re-heated but you may find they will separate as they cool; this can be remedied by whisking the soup with a wire whisk as it re-heats.

Cream of celery soup
Made at home with fresh ingredients this can be a very delicious soup indeed.
Serves 4–6.
1 large heart celery
2 tablespoons finely chopped celery leaves
1 medium onion
1 oz butter
2 pints chicken stock
3 bay leaves
sprig thyme (or ½ teaspoon dried thyme)
salt and freshly ground black pepper
3 tablespoons flour;
¼ pint milk
3 tablespoons double cream

Trim off the leaves of the celery and the bottom of the stalk. Cut the stalks into 1 inch pieces and wash them well. Peel and finely chop the onion.

Melt the butter in a large saucepan, add the onion and celery and cook over a low heat until the onion is soft and transparent. Add the stock, bay leaves and thyme, season with salt and freshly ground black pepper and simmer for about 45 minutes until the celery is absolutely tender. Remove the bay leaves and thyme sprig. Purée the soup though a food mill or in an electric blender or food processor and return it to a clean pan.

Mix the flour and milk to a smooth paste, add them to the celery purée and mix well. Bring to the boil, stirring all the time and simmer for five minutes. Blend in the cream and serve the soup garnished with the finely chopped celery leaves.

Cream of artichoke soup (Palestine Soup)
Serves 6
2 lb Jerusalem artichokes
2 onions
2 oz butter
2 pints chicken stock
½ pint single cream (or use half milk and half cream)
salt and freshly ground black pepper
pinch ground nutmeg

Peel the artichokes as above and drop them, roughly chopped, into water to which some lemon juice has been added. Peel and roughly chop the onions. Melt the butter in a large saucepan, add the onion and cook over a low heat until the onions are soft and transparent. Drain the artichokes, add them to the onions and cook, stirring frequently, until all the butter has been absorbed into the vegetables. Add the stock, bring to the boil, cover and simmer for about 20 minutes or until the artichokes are tender. Purée the artichokes in an electric liquidiser, through a food mill or in a food processor and return them to a clean pan. Add the cream, season with salt, pepper and nutmeg and heat through without boiling.

Index